SKY OVER LIBERTY FARM

Twin Projects: Brazil
"Sky Over Liberty Farm" is the graphic, non-fiction part
of the "Twin Projects: Brazil." The fiction part is the novel
"Liberty Farm: A Family Portrait."

SKY OVER LIBERTY FARM

IZAI AMORIM

First edition: 2014
Published by Izai Amorim

ISBN Numbers:
978-1502591302 — Softcover (Amazon distribution)
978-3982165653 — Softcover (Ingram distribution)

Photographs, text, and book design by Izai Amorim

Author's website:
www.izaiamorim.com

Book website:
www.skyoverlibertyfarm.izaiamorim.com

Author's mailing list:
www.mailinglist.izaiamorim.com

In memory of my great-grandparents Alfredo and Julia

In Brazil's northeast – 15 degrees south of the Equator,
40 degrees west of Greenwich – there is a place called
Liberty Farm. The landscape has changed over time
but the sky remains the same. Many generations have
enjoyed its beauty. Now it's your turn!

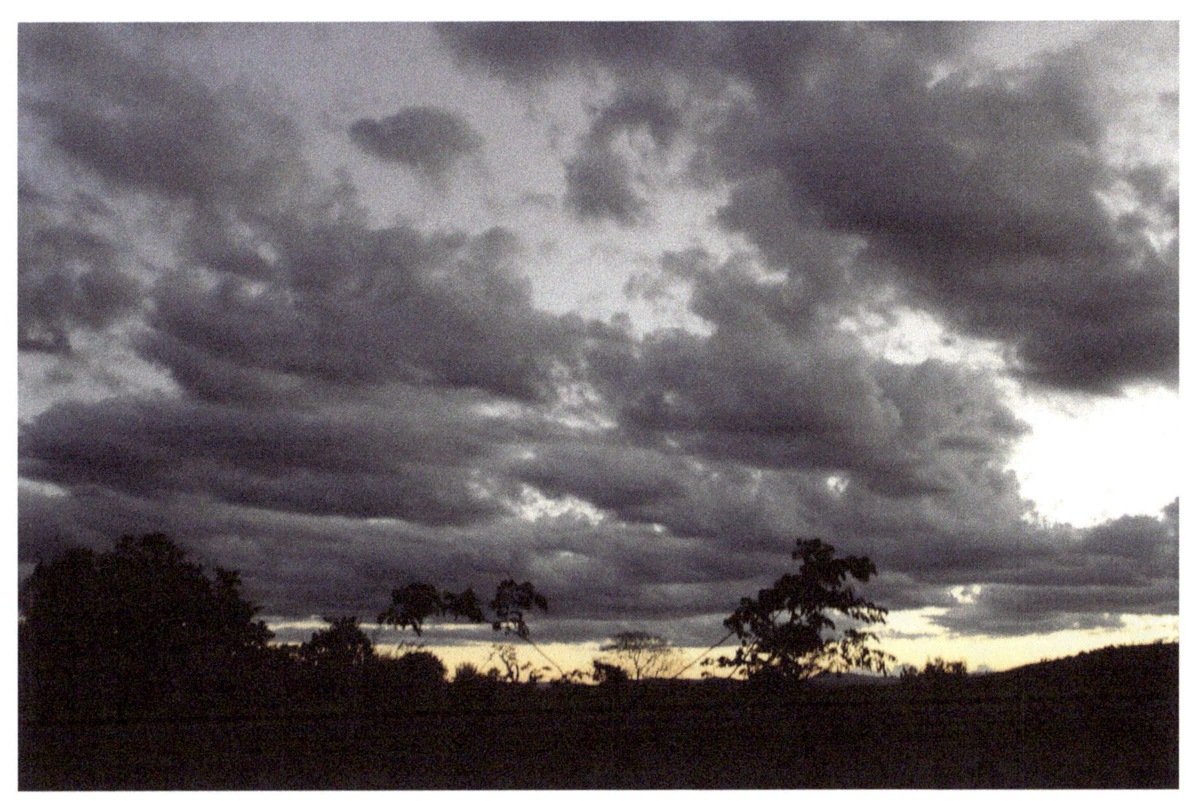

Sky Over Liberty Farm

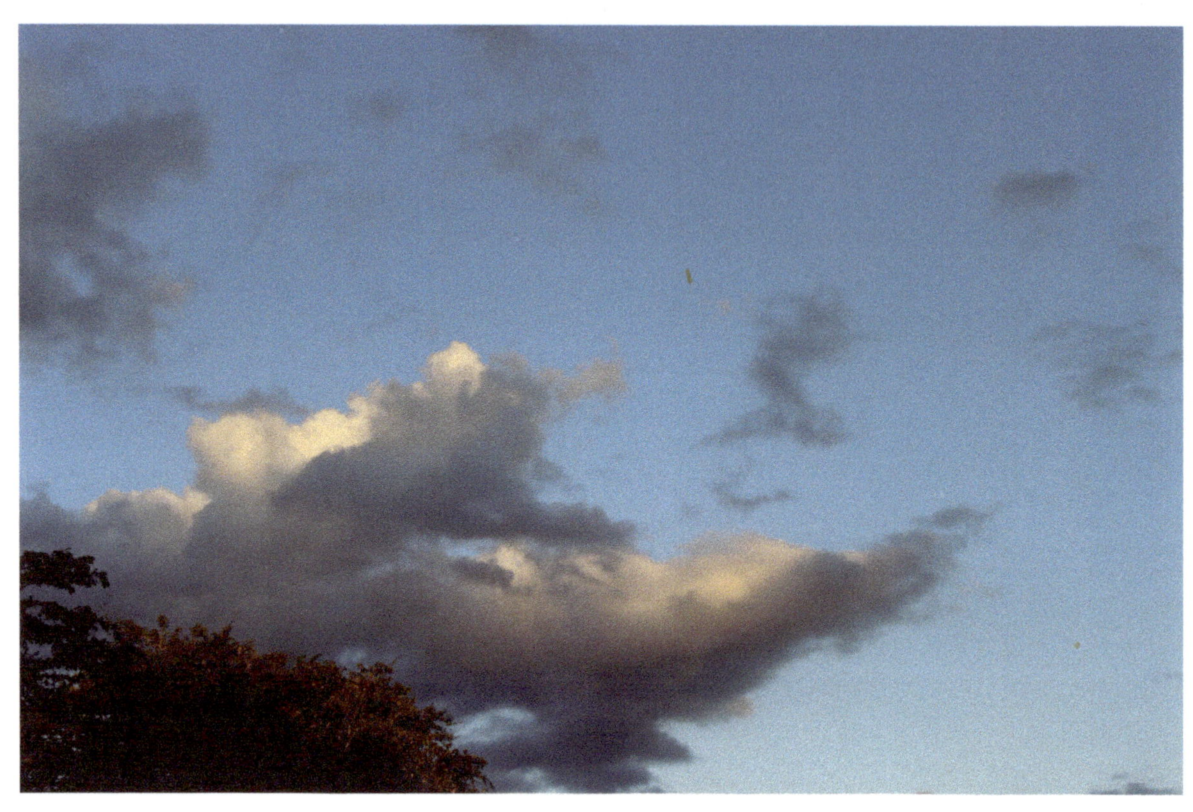

Izai Amorim

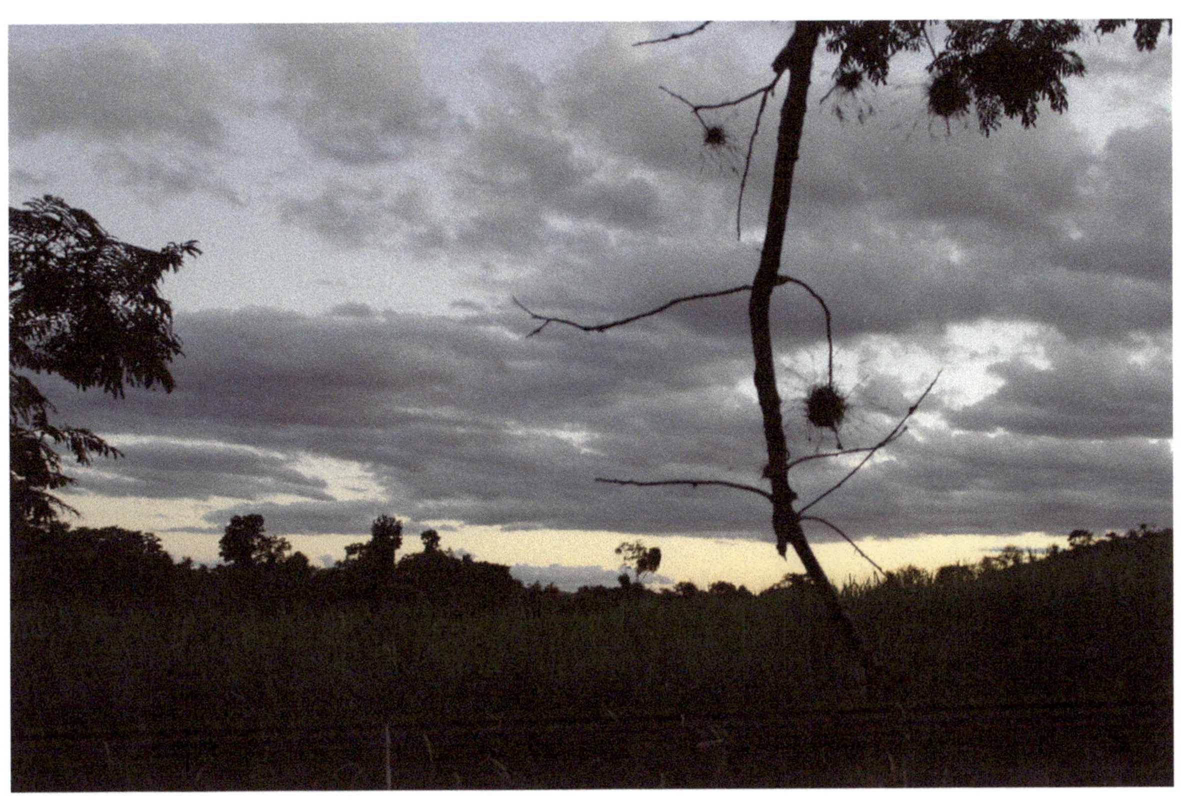

Sky Over Liberty Farm

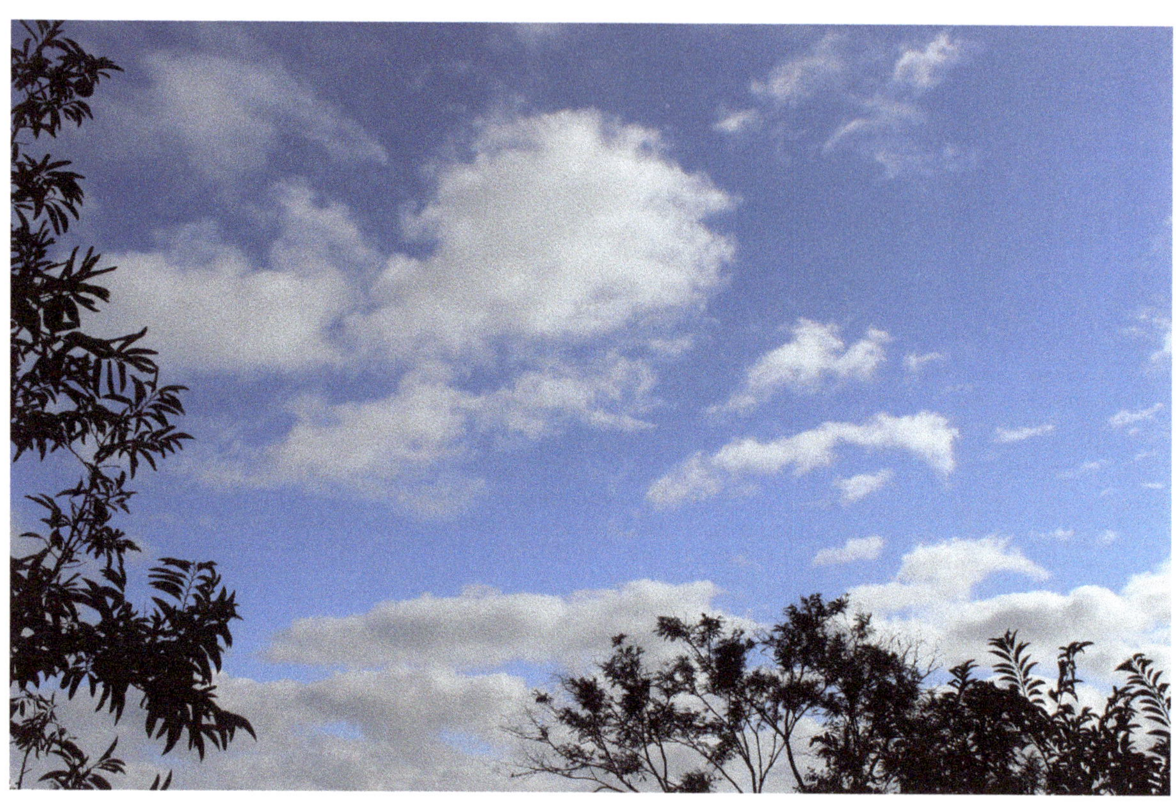

Izai Amorim

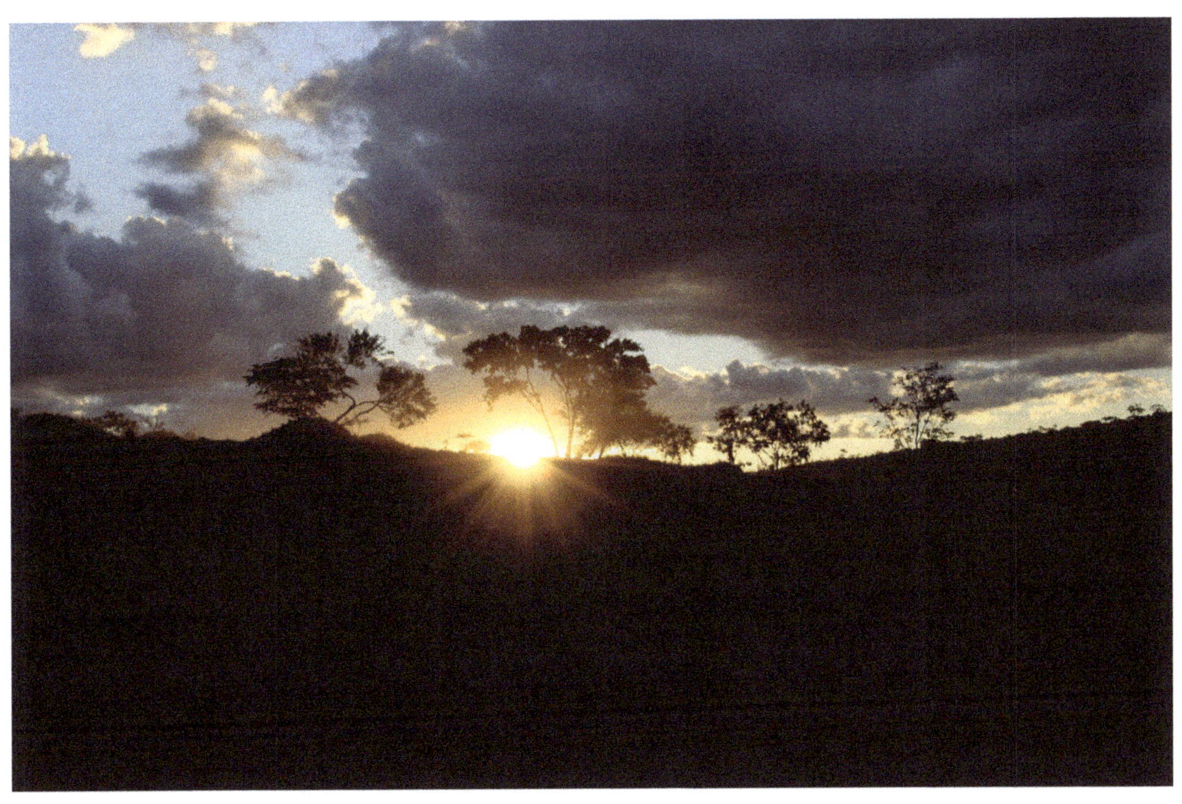

Sky Over Liberty Farm

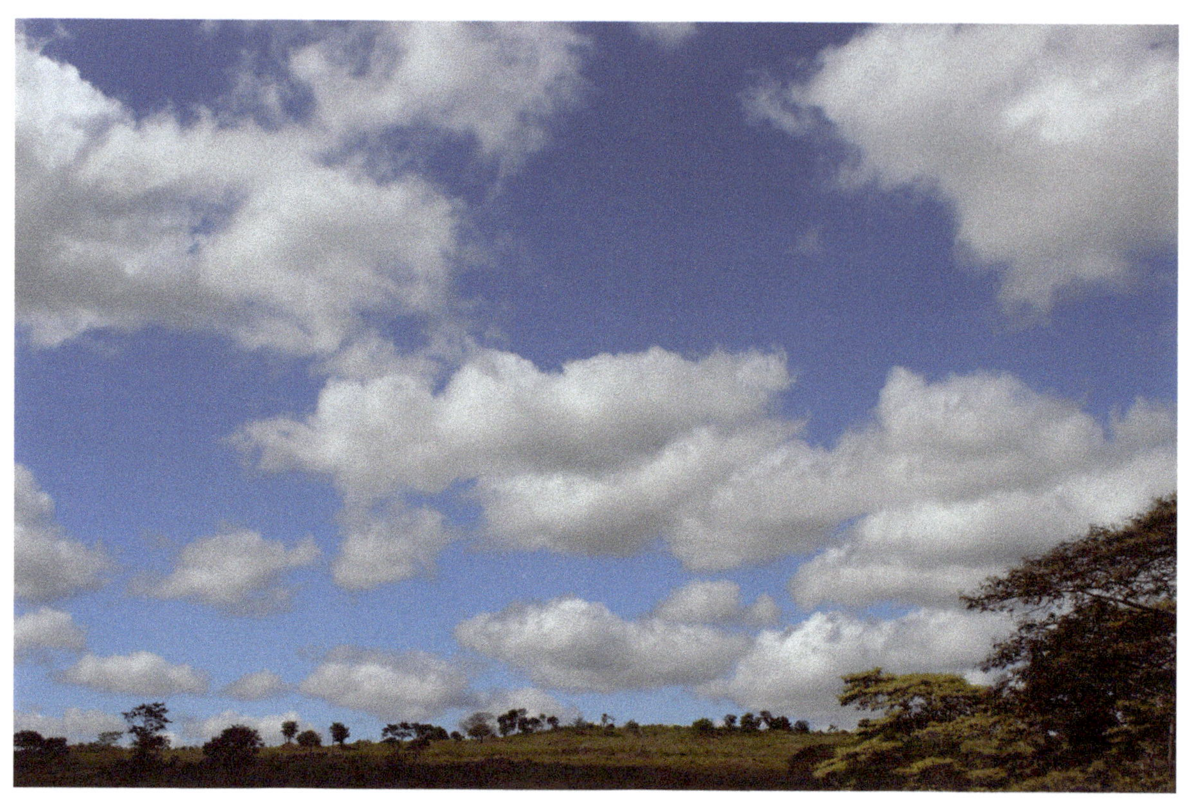

Izai Amorim

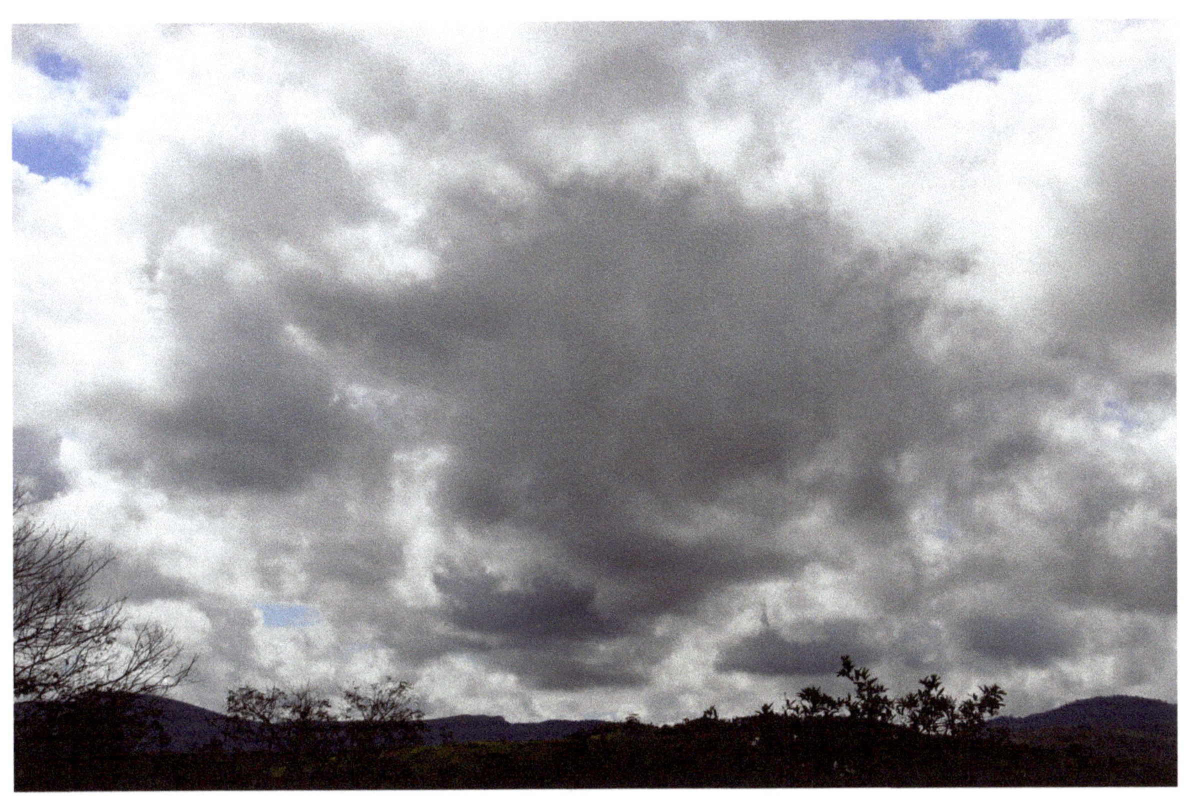

Sky Over Liberty Farm

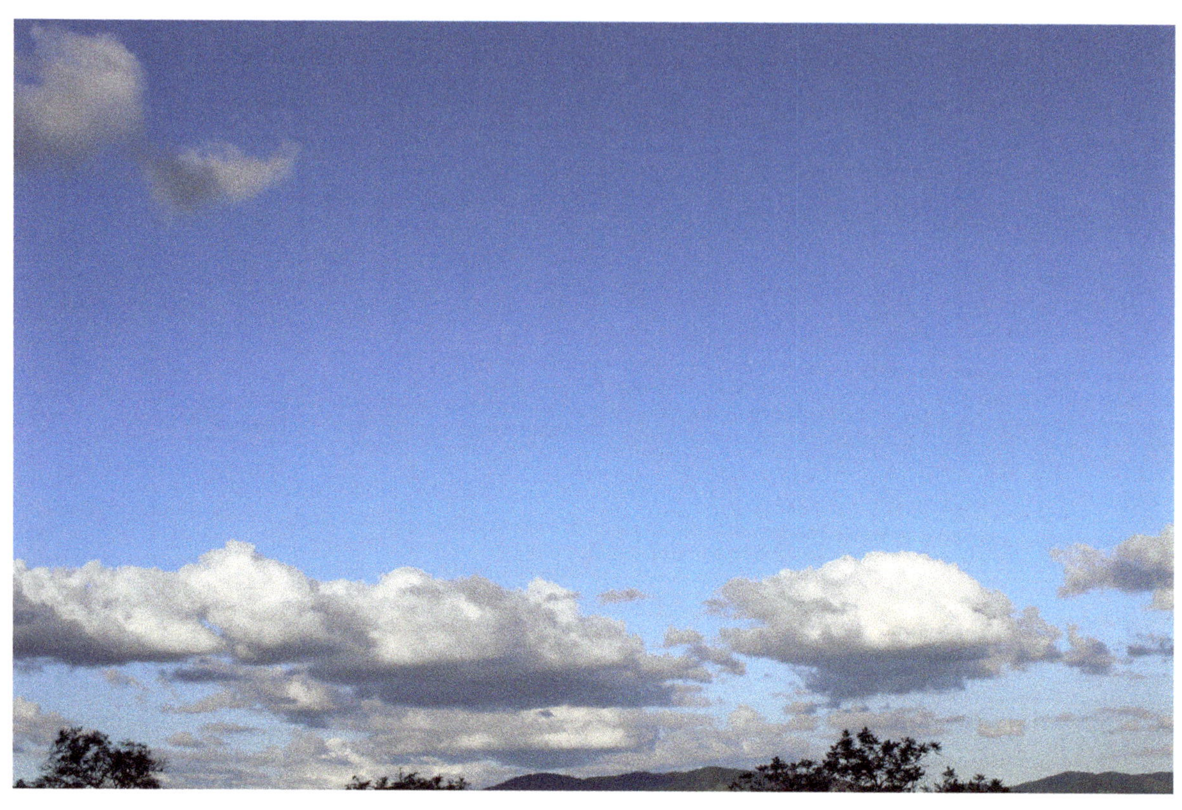

Izai Amorim

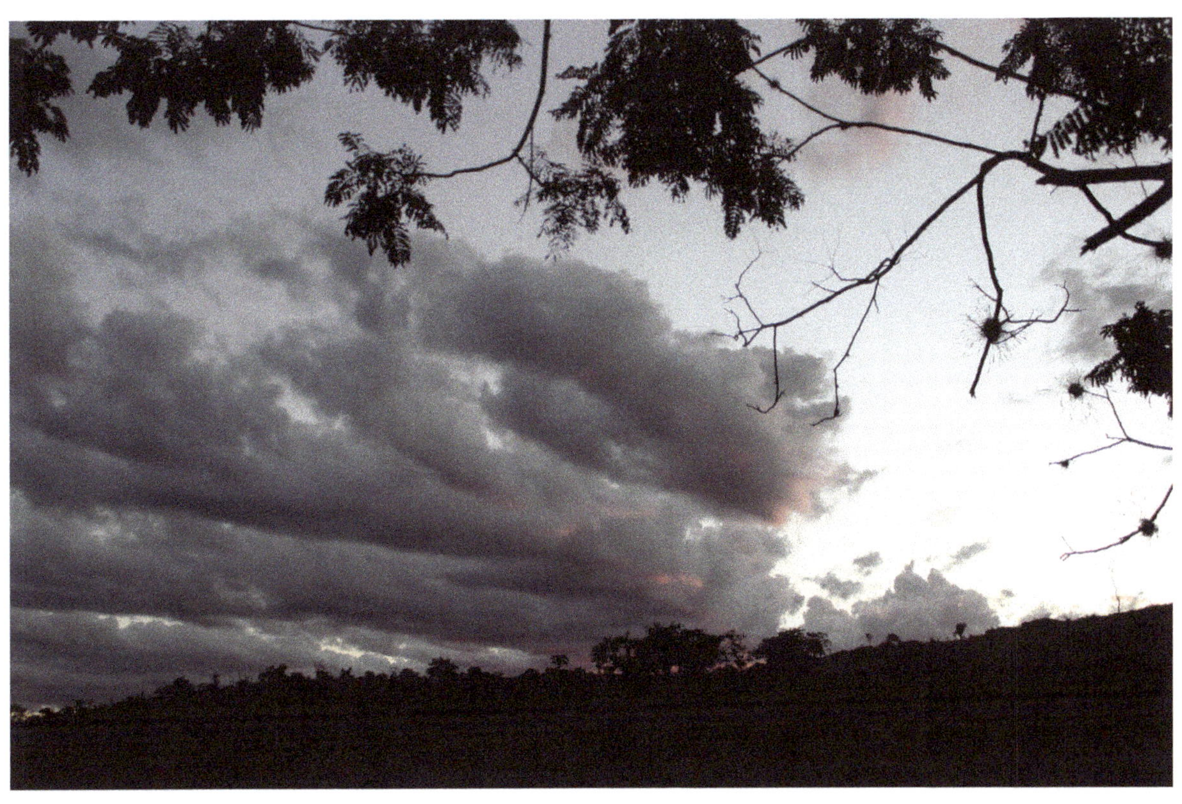

Sky Over Liberty Farm

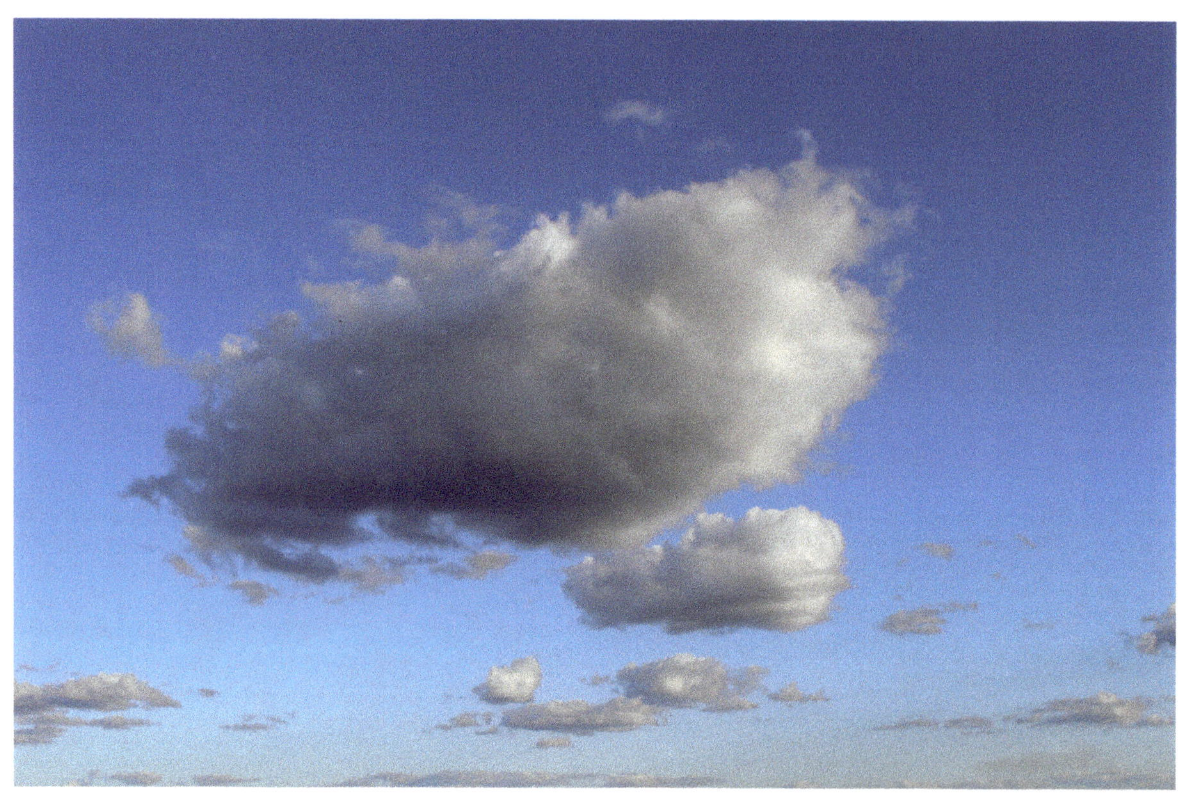

Izai Amorim

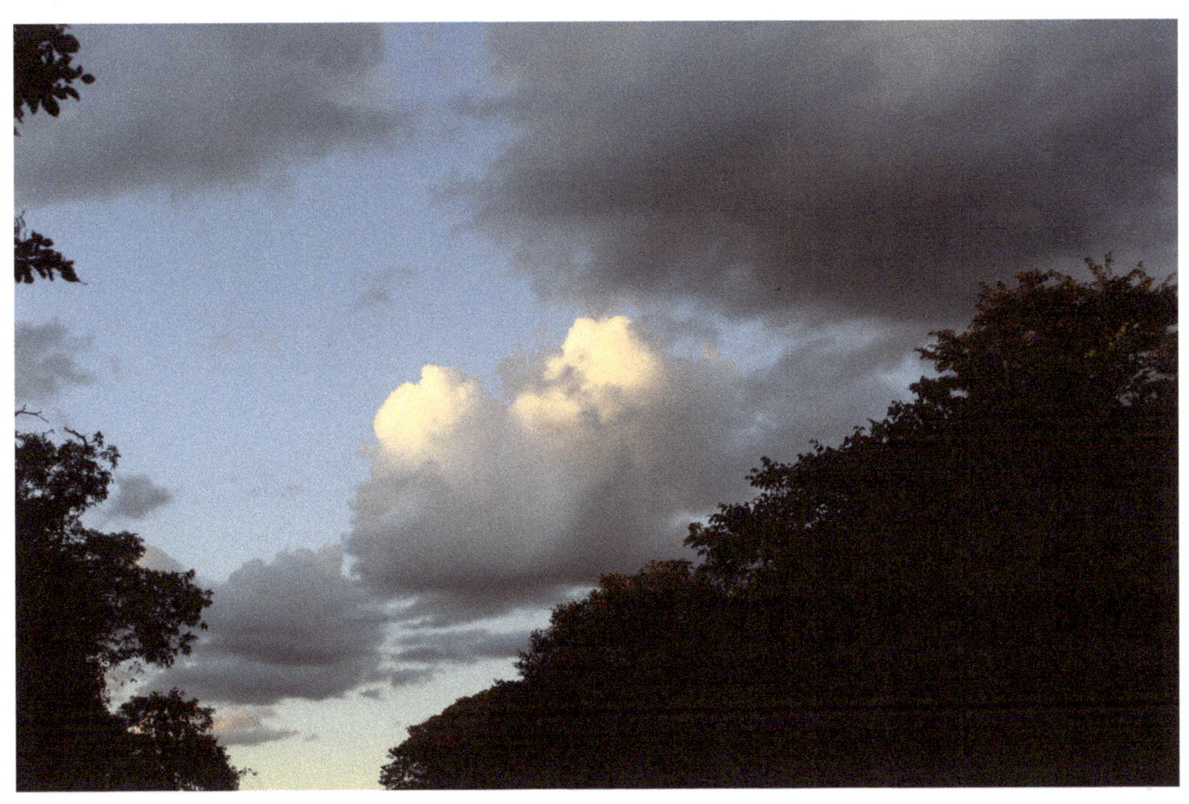

Sky Over Liberty Farm

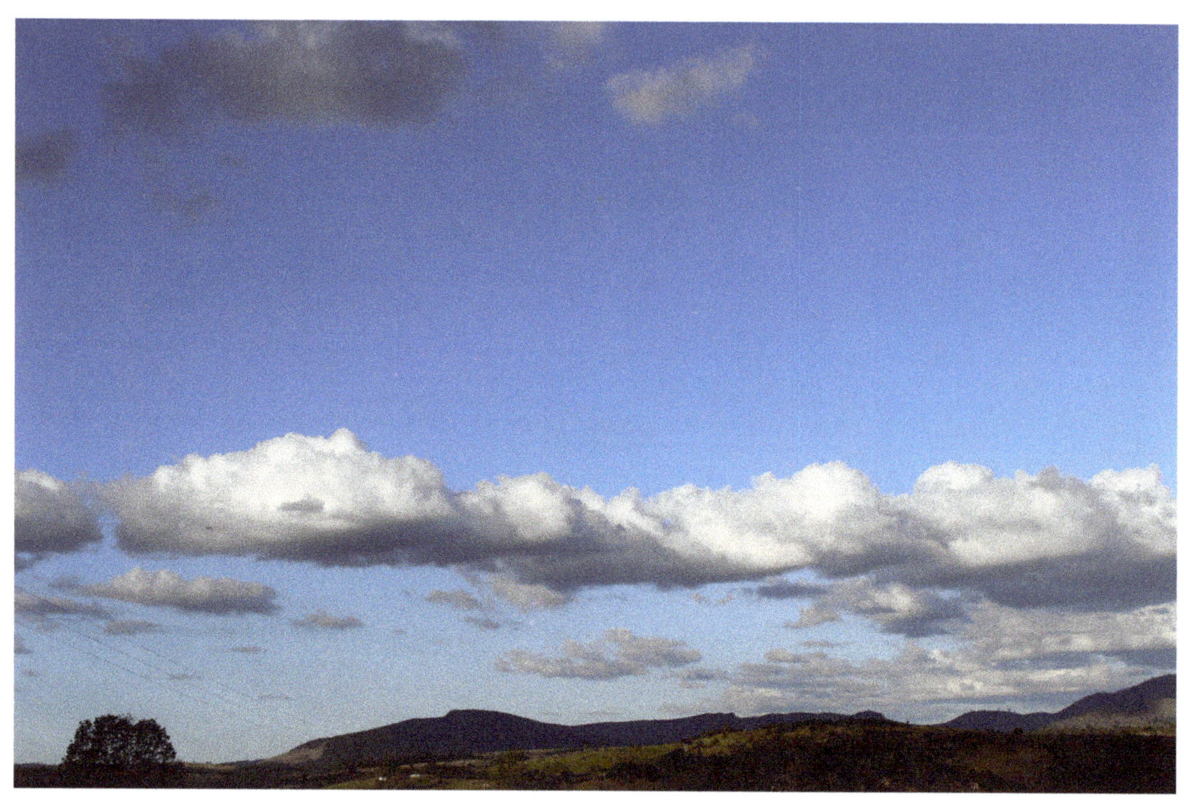

Izai Amorim

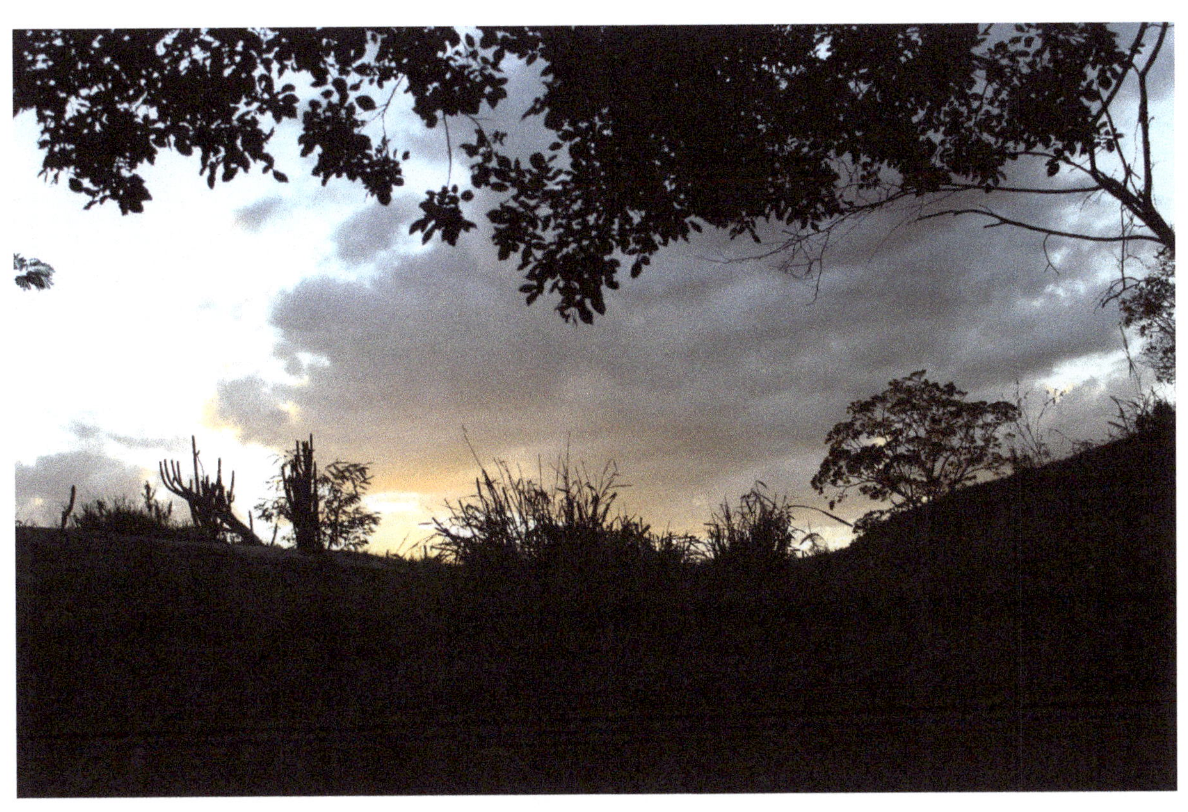

Sky Over Liberty Farm

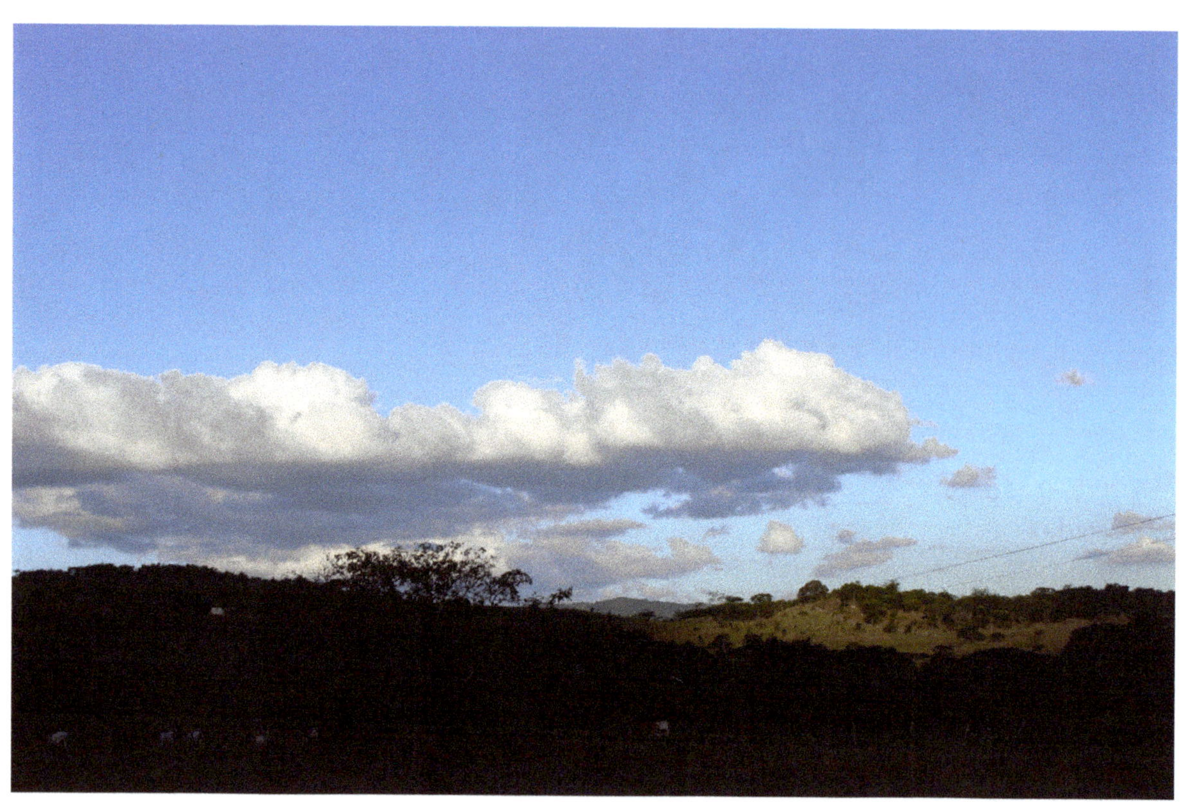

Izai Amorim

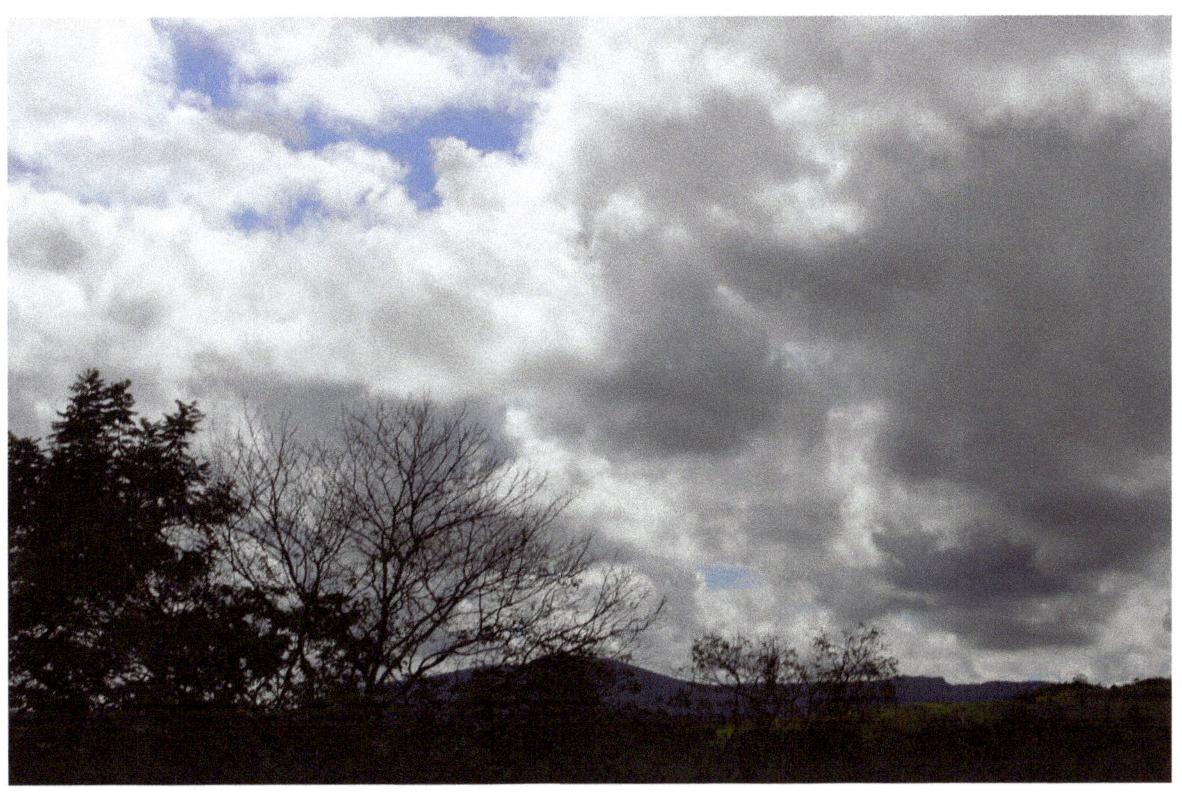

Sky Over Liberty Farm

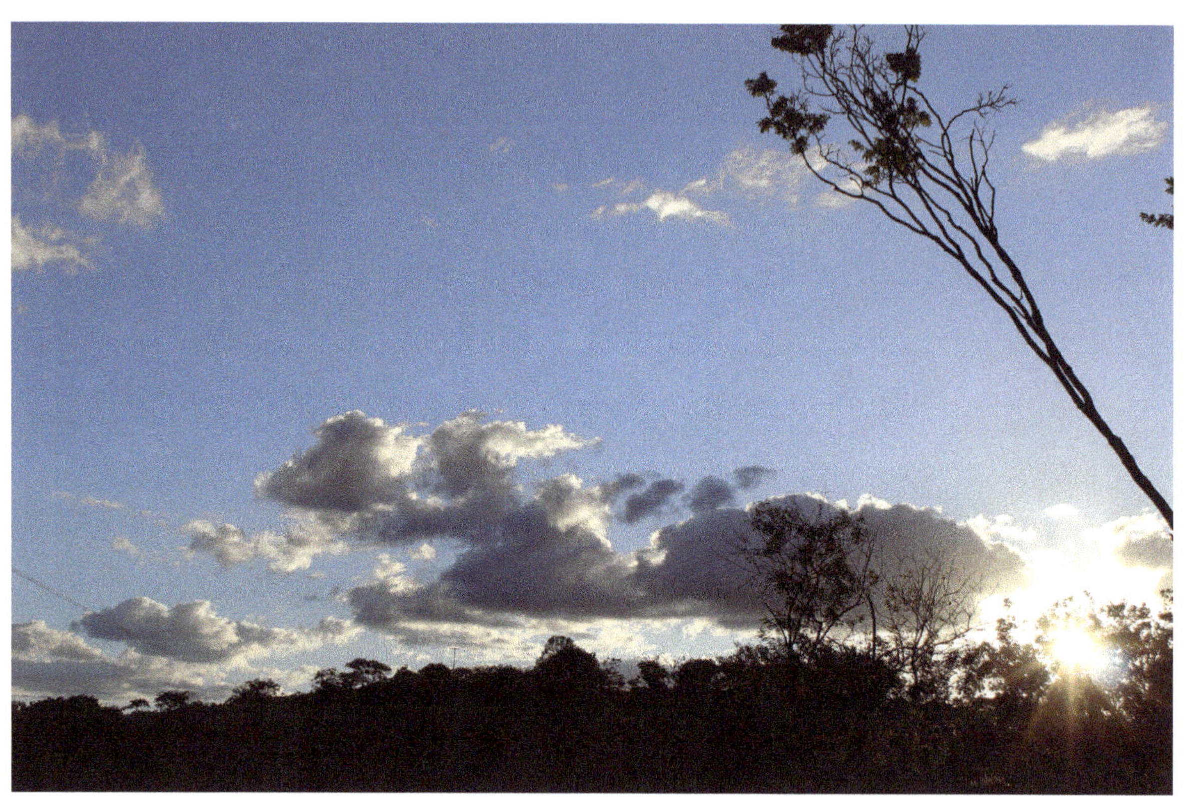

Izai Amorim

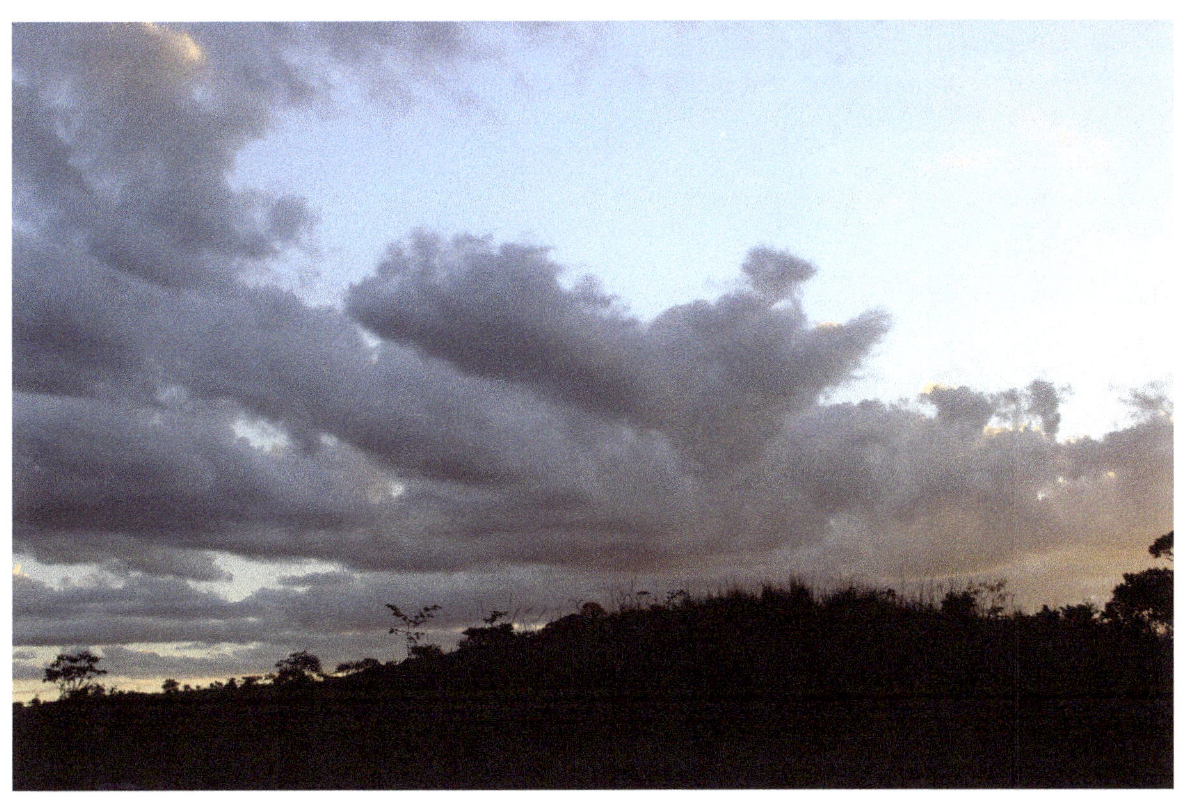

Sky Over Liberty Farm

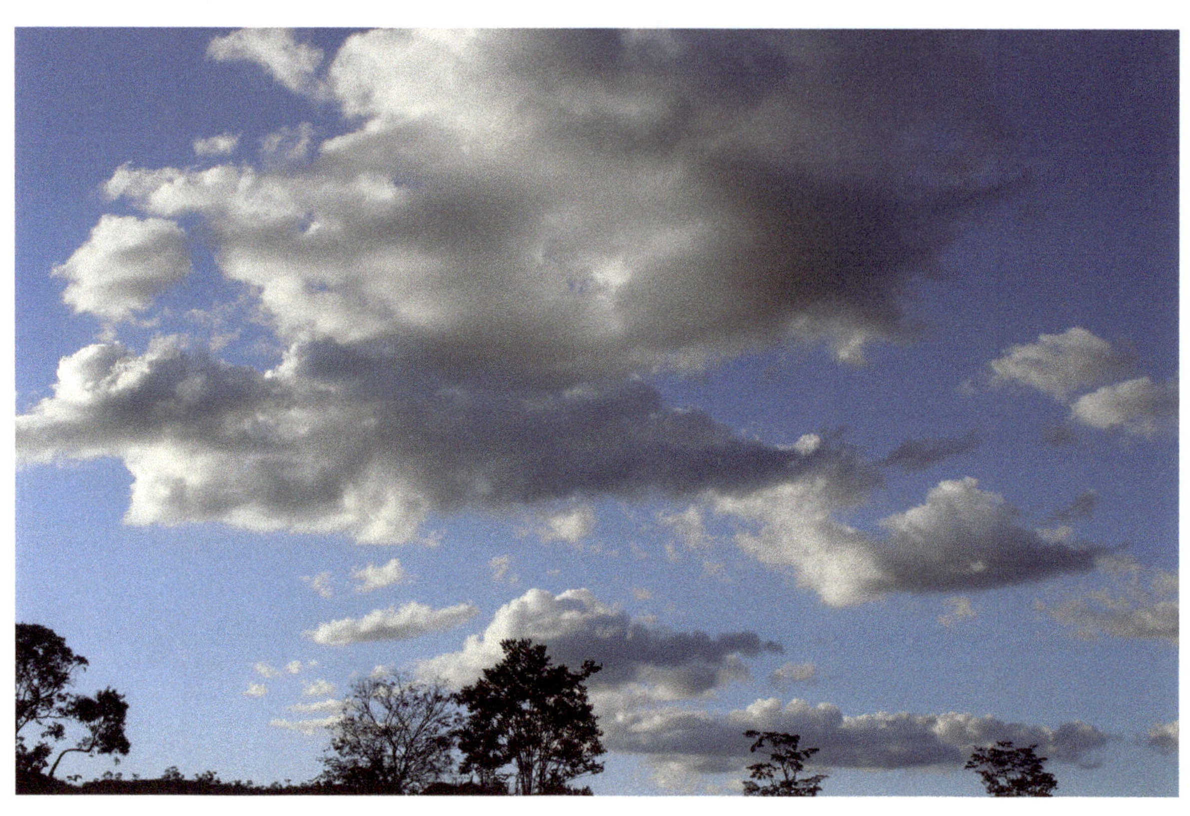

Izai Amorim

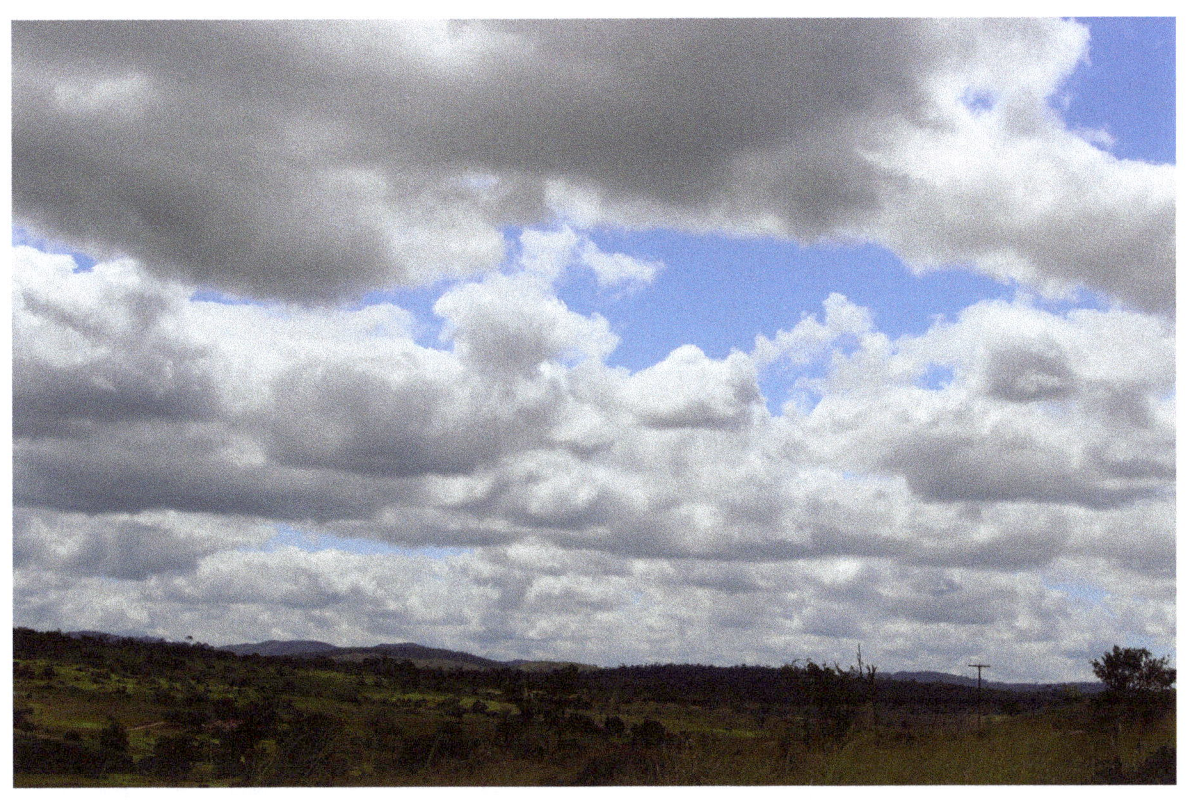

Sky Over Liberty Farm

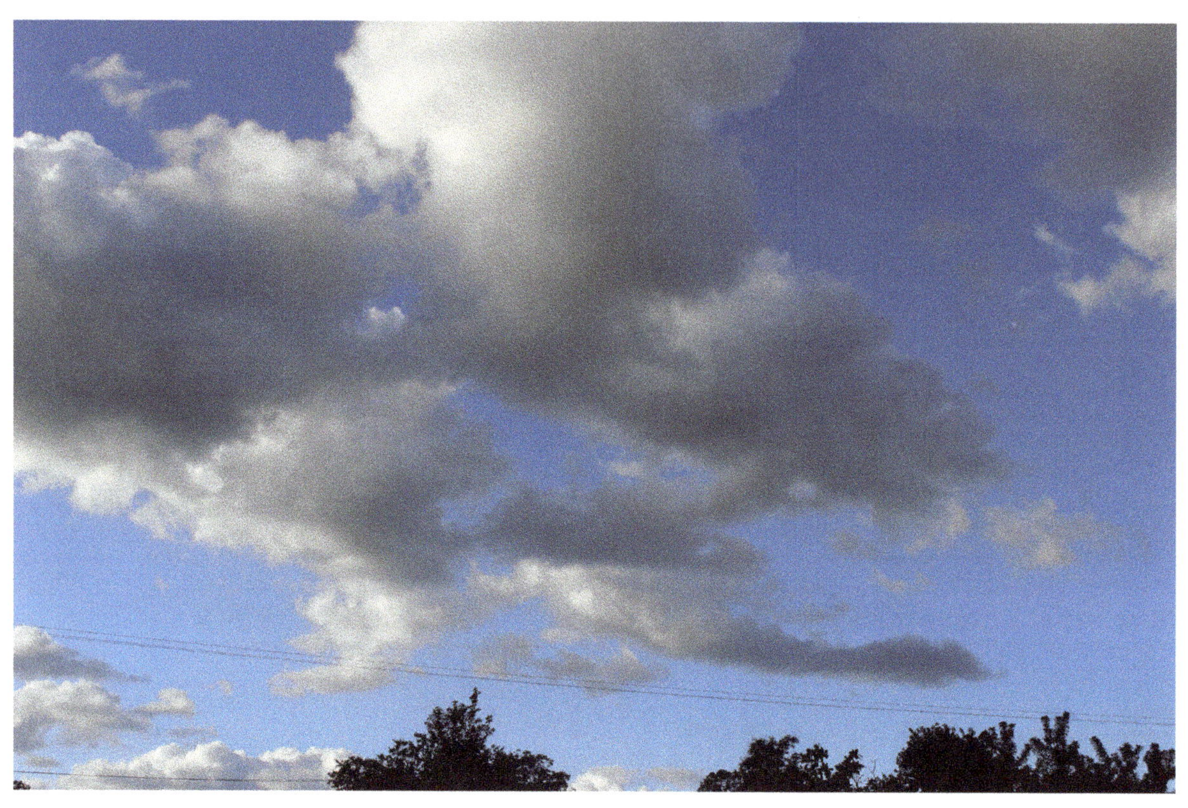

Izai Amorim

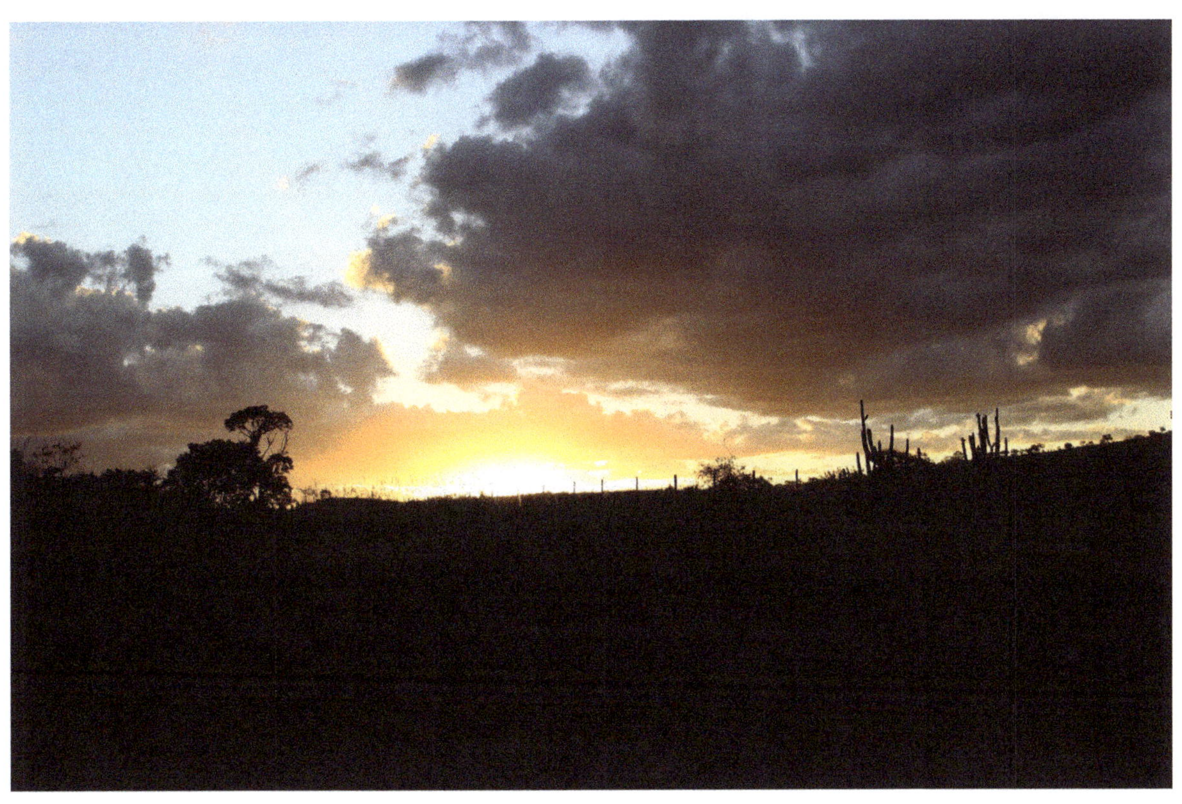

Sky Over Liberty Farm

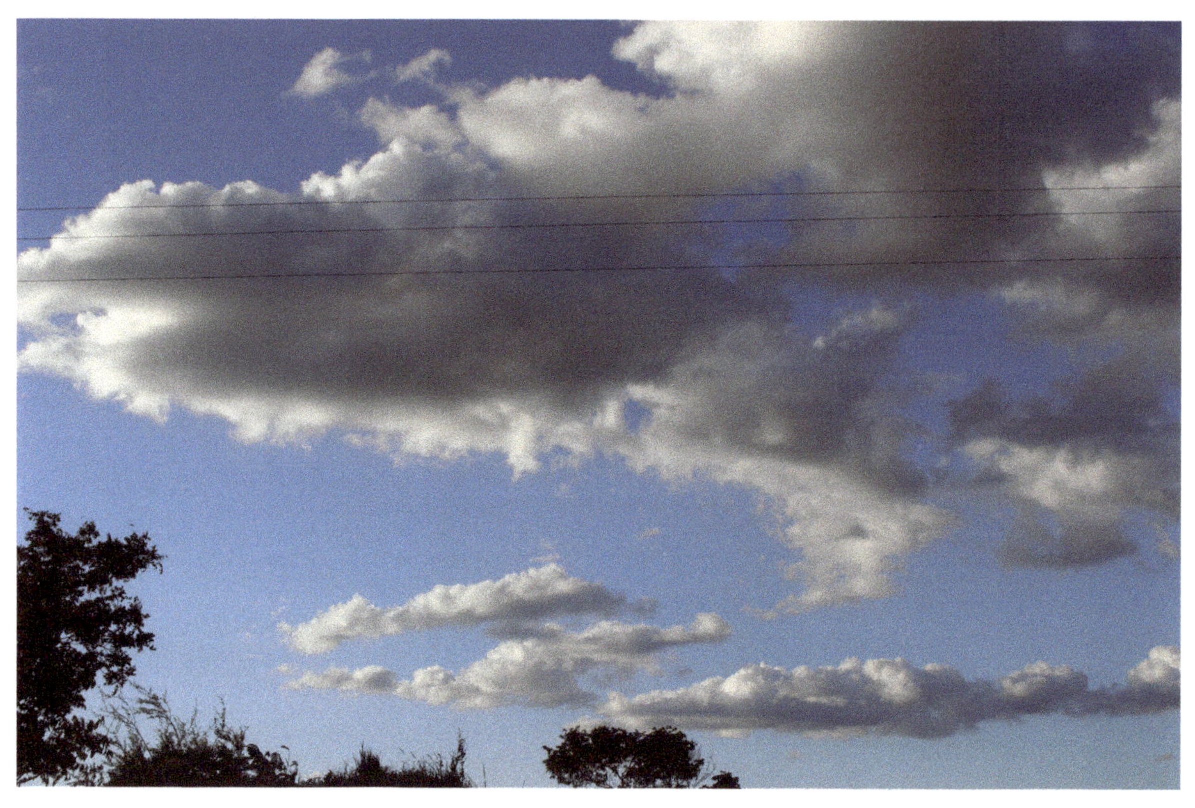

22

Izai Amorim

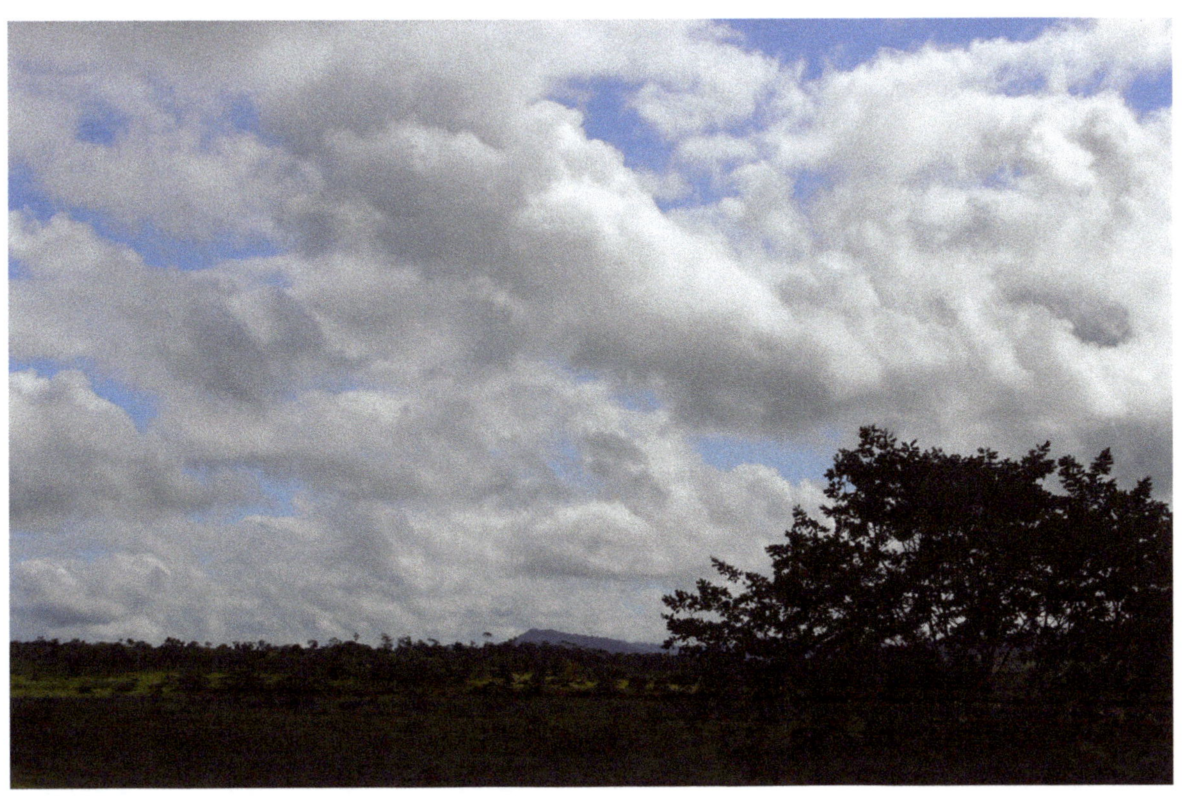

Sky Over Liberty Farm

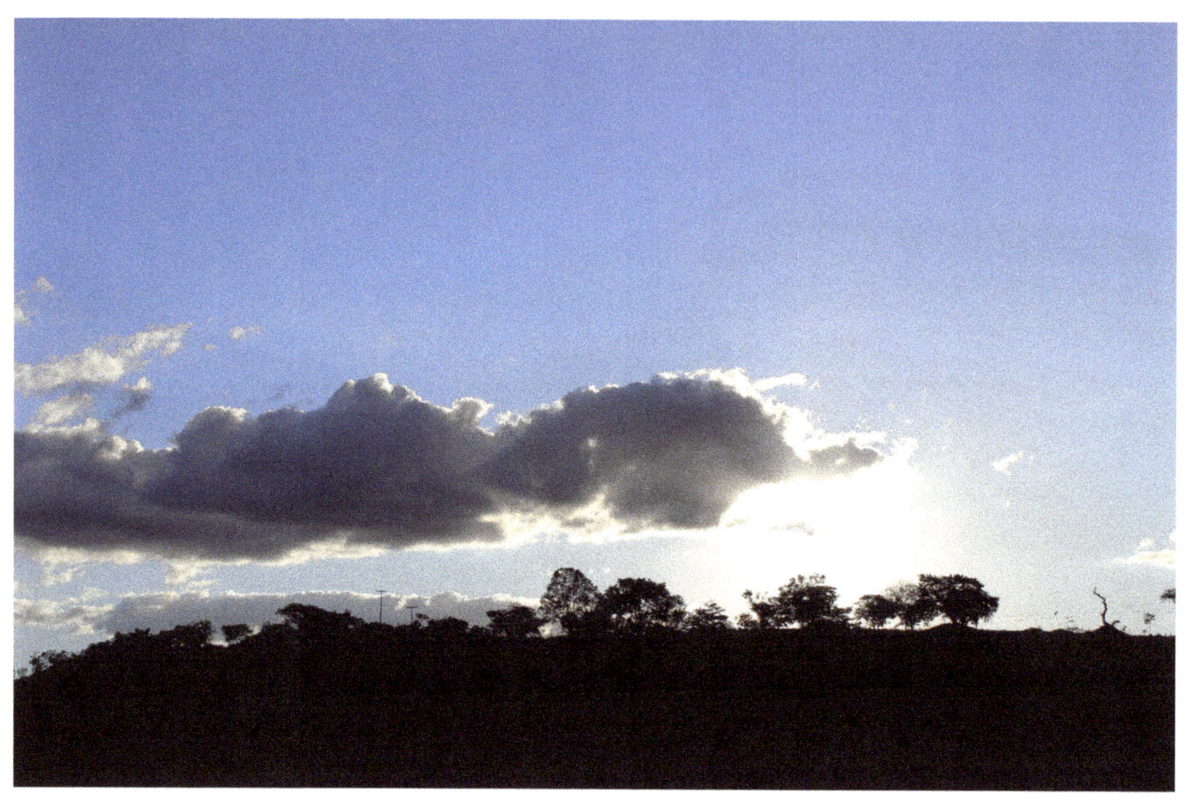

Izai Amorim

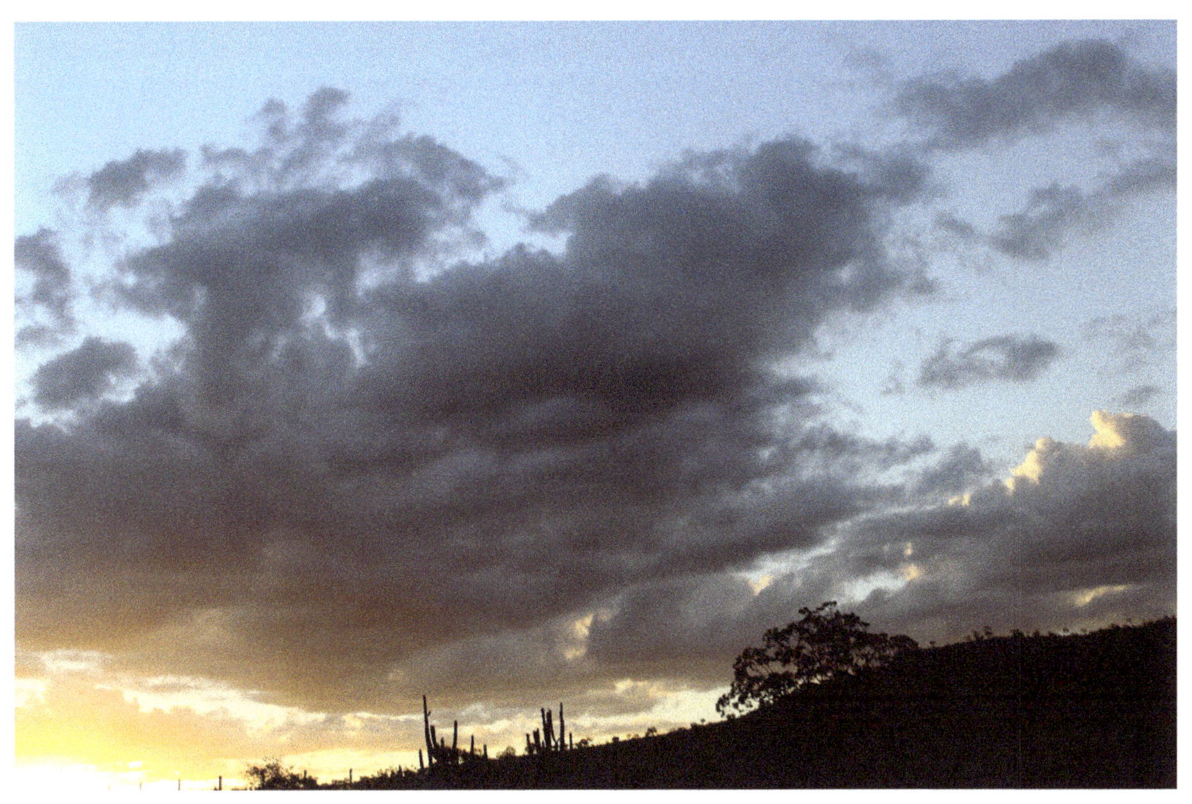

Sky Over Liberty Farm

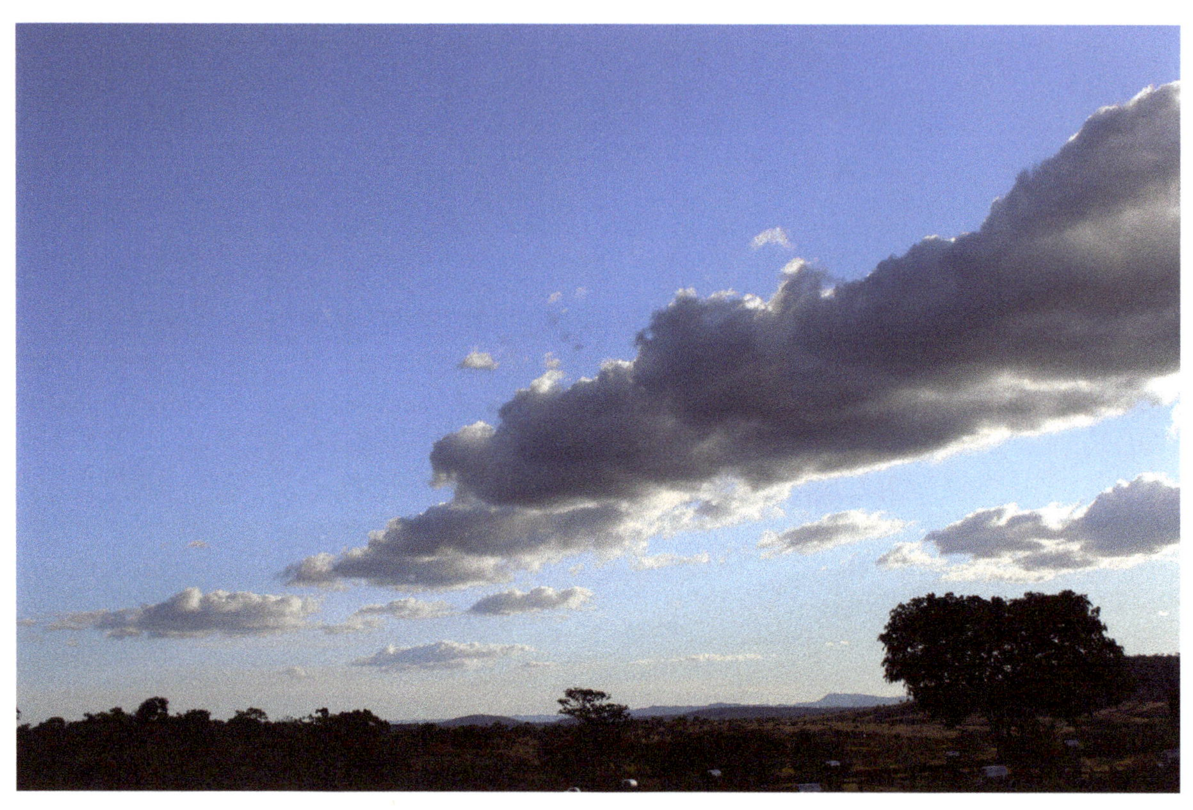

Izai Amorim

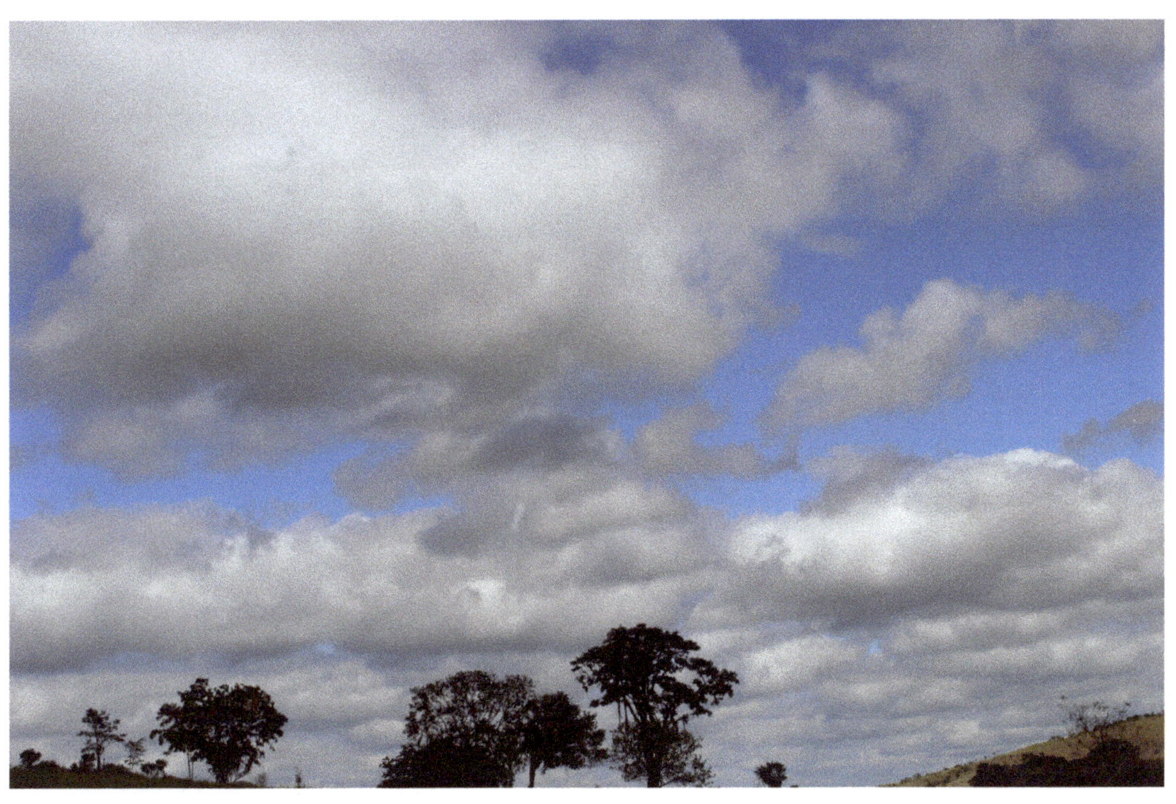

Sky Over Liberty Farm

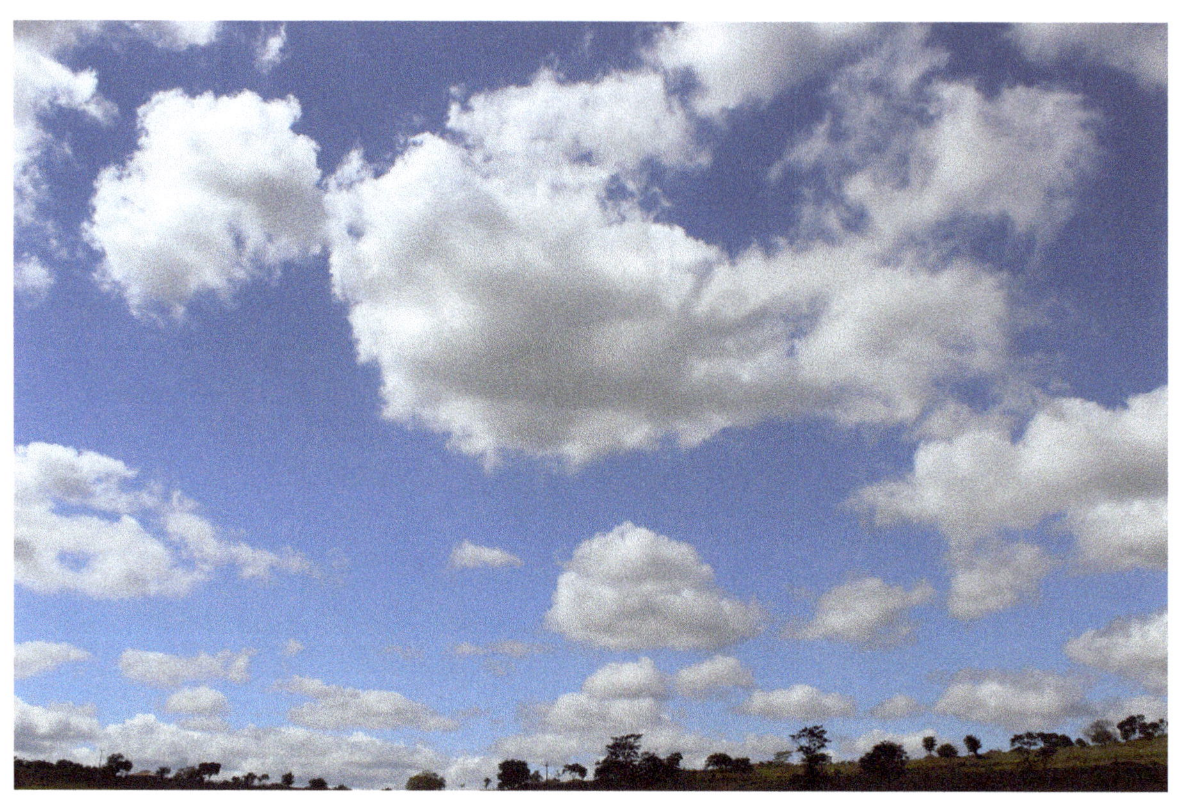

Izai Amorim

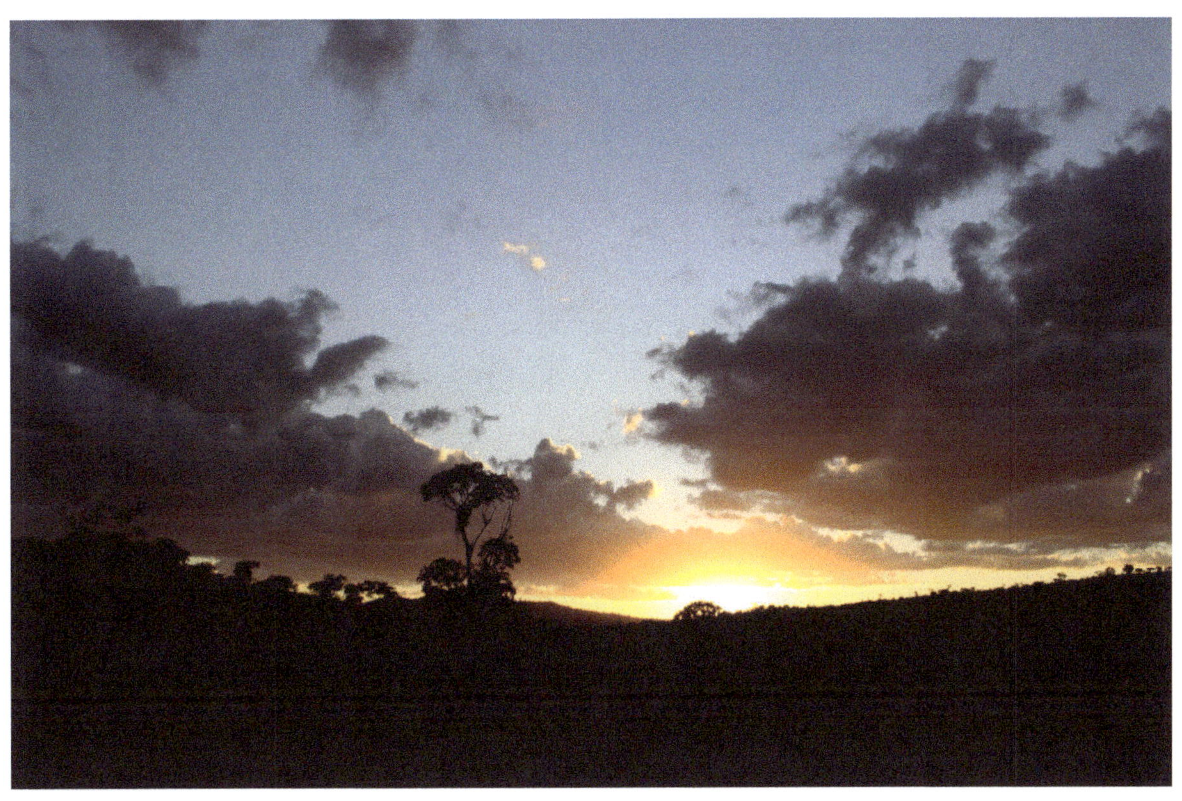

Sky Over Liberty Farm

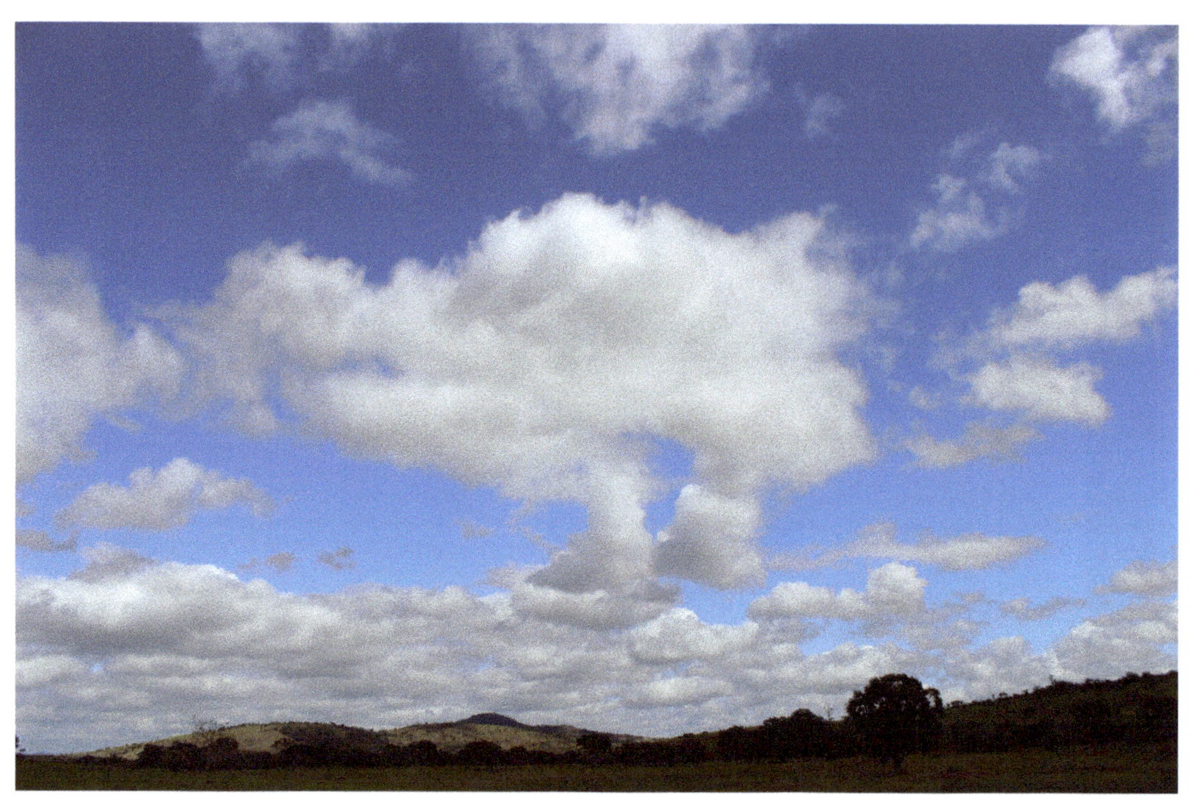

Izai Amorim

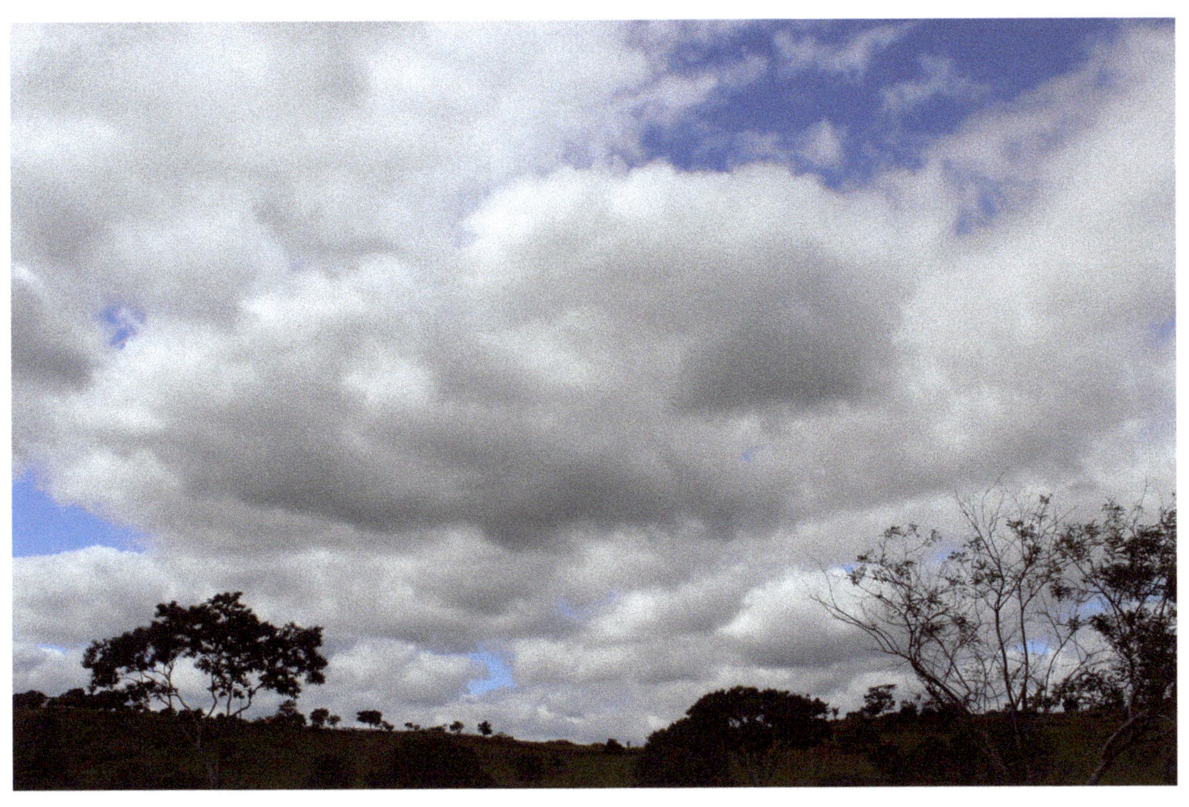

Sky Over Liberty Farm

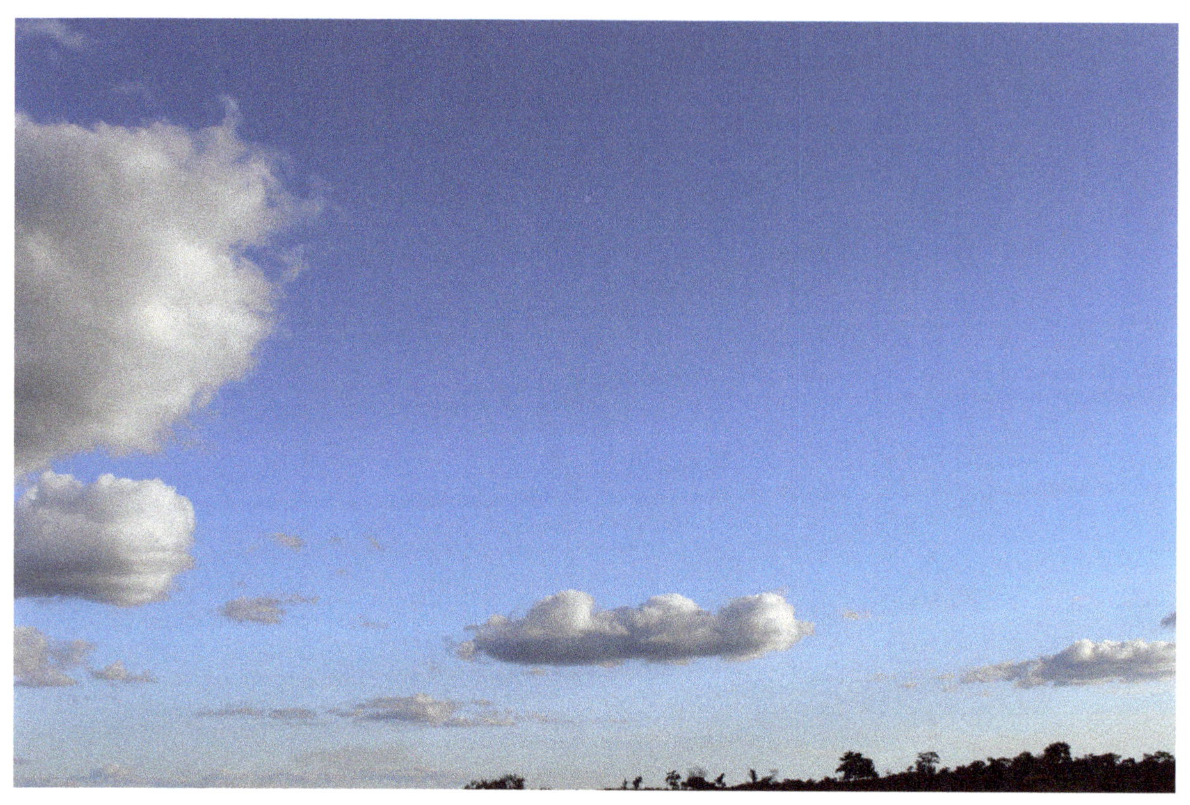

Izai Amorim

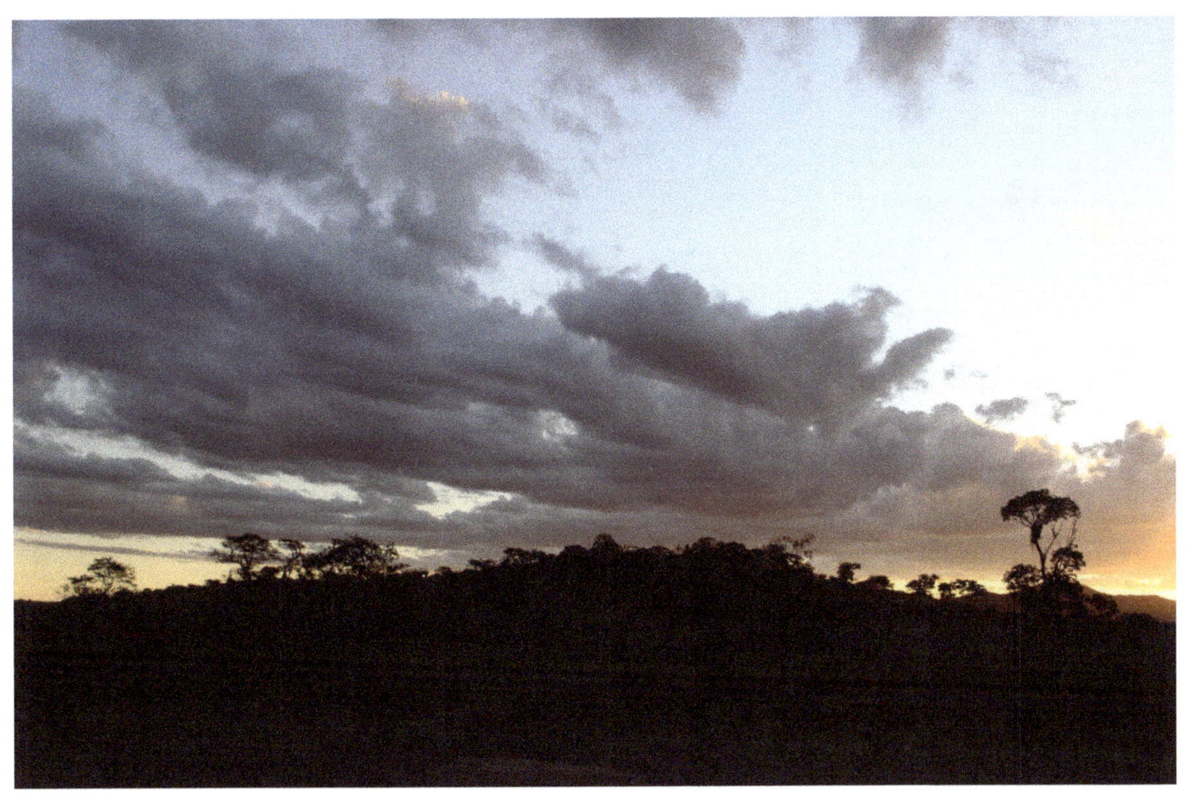

Sky Over Liberty Farm

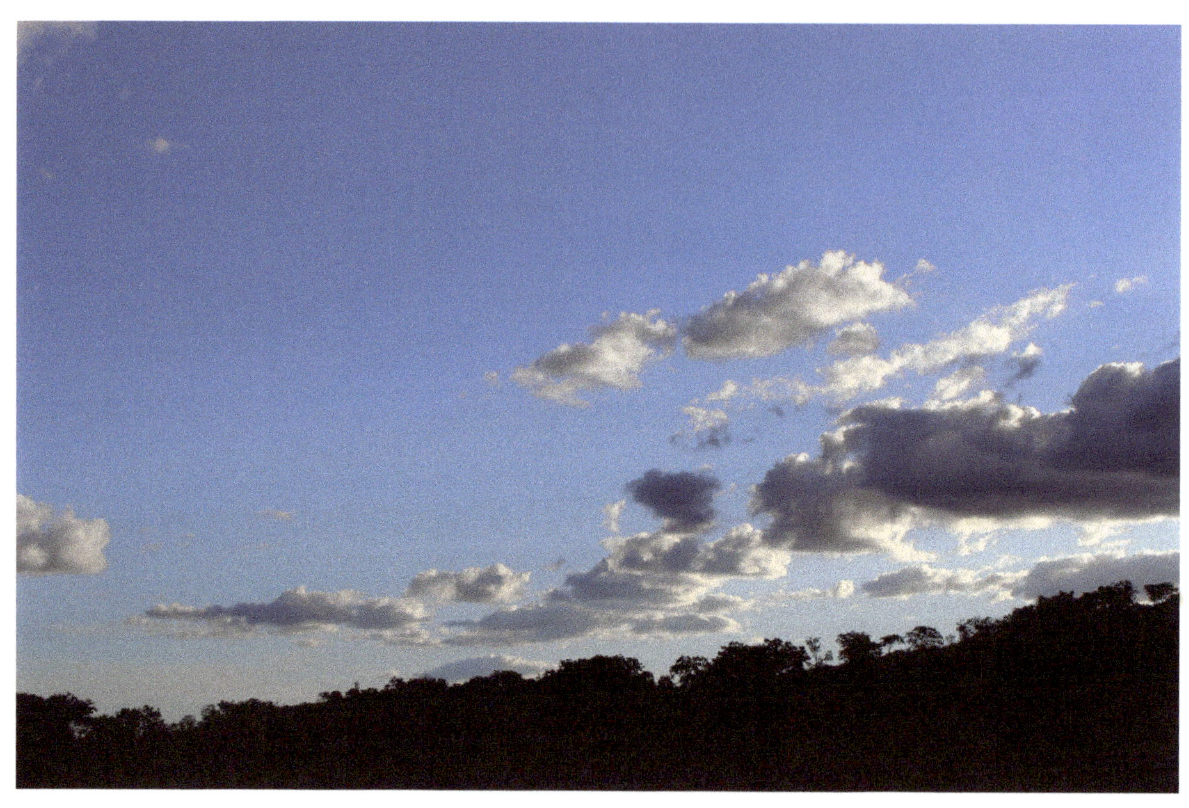

Izai Amorim

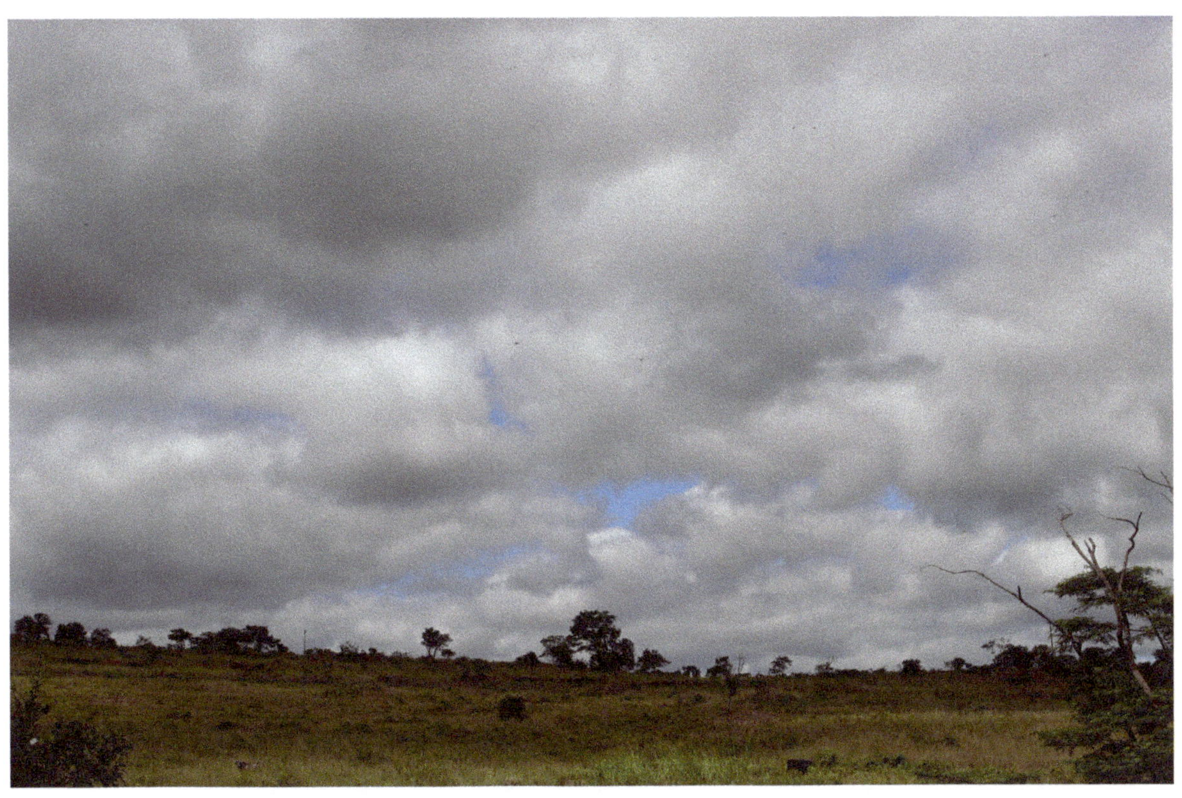

Sky Over Liberty Farm

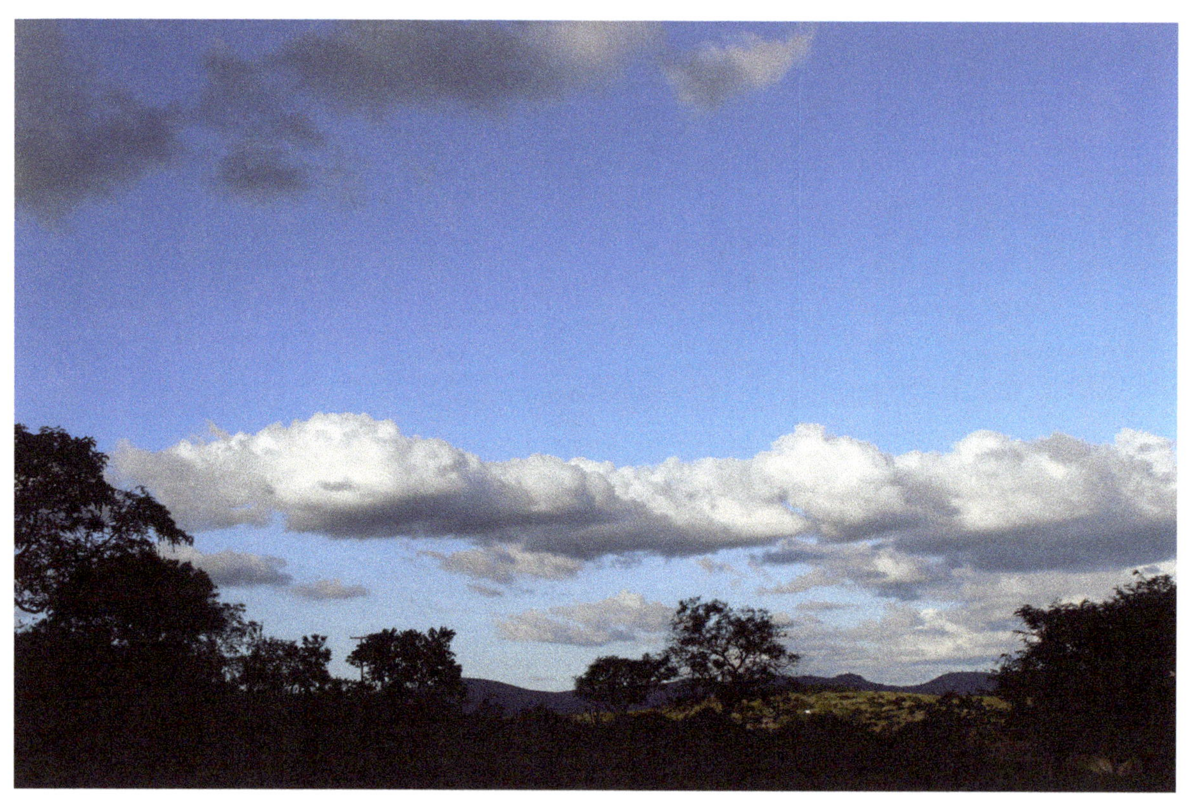

Izai Amorim

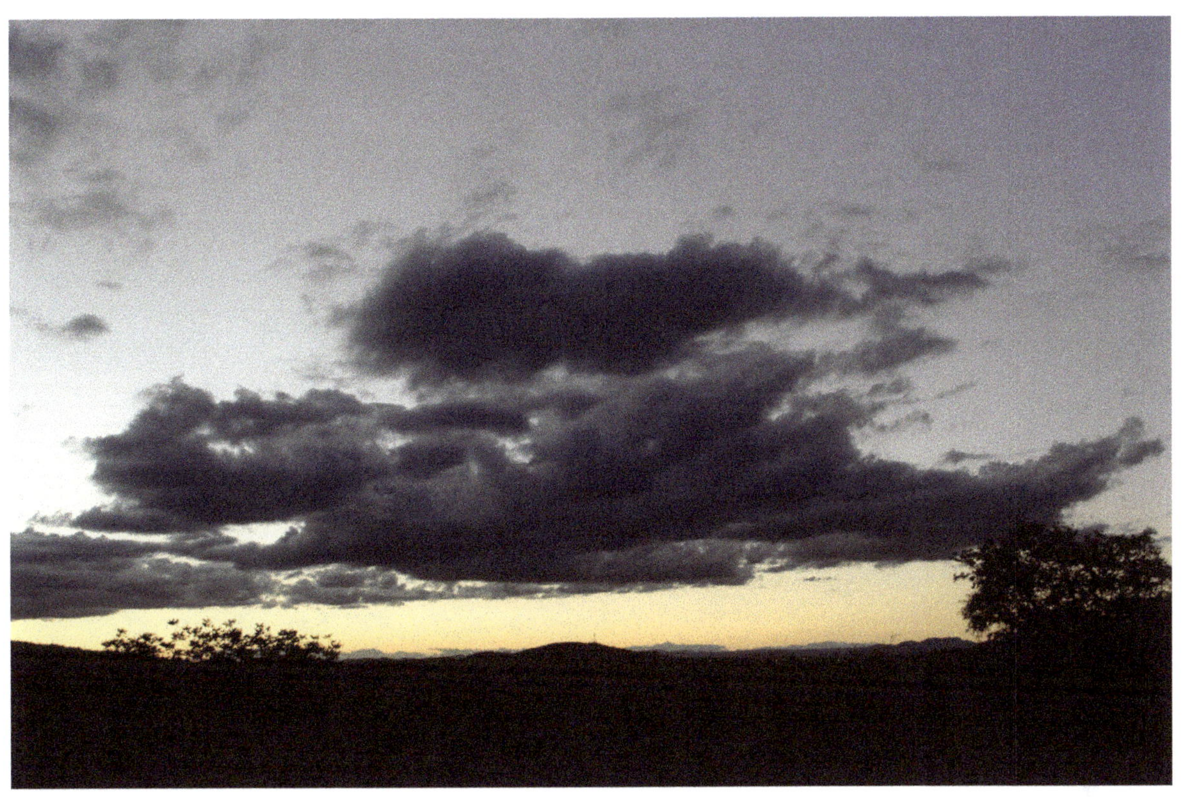

Sky Over Liberty Farm   37

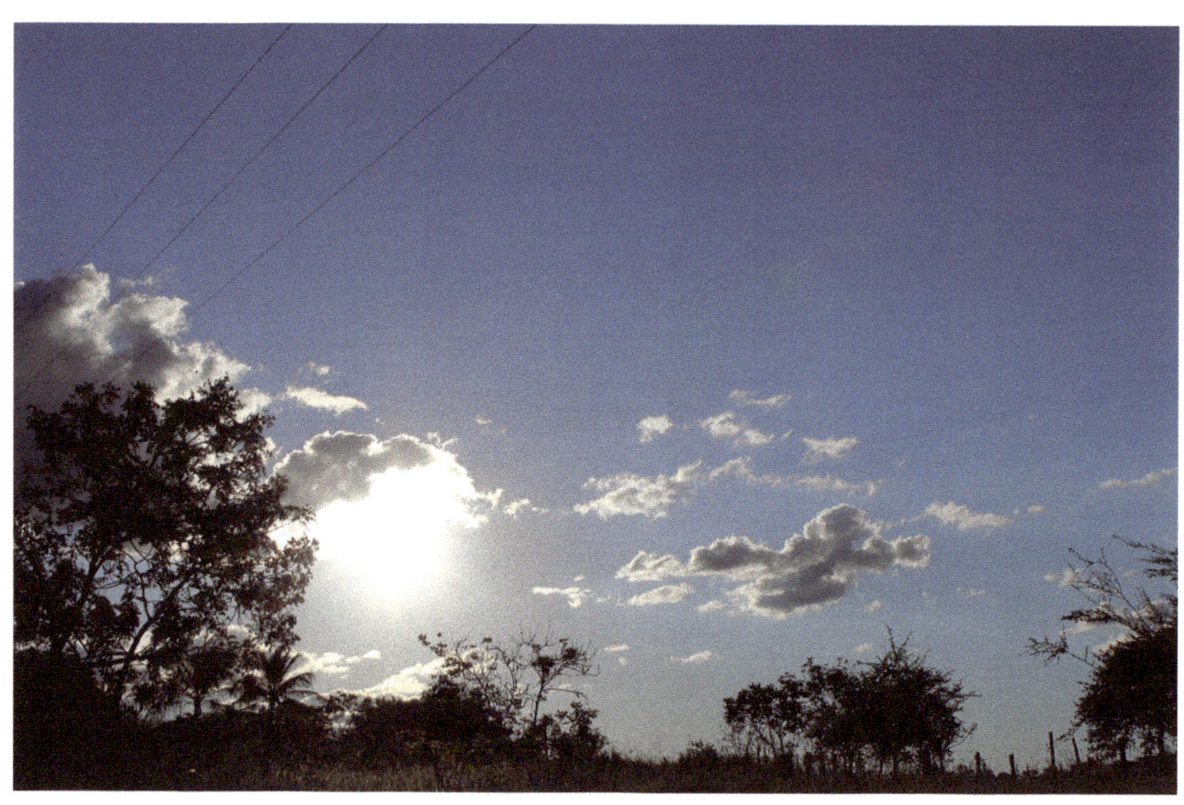

38

Izai Amorim

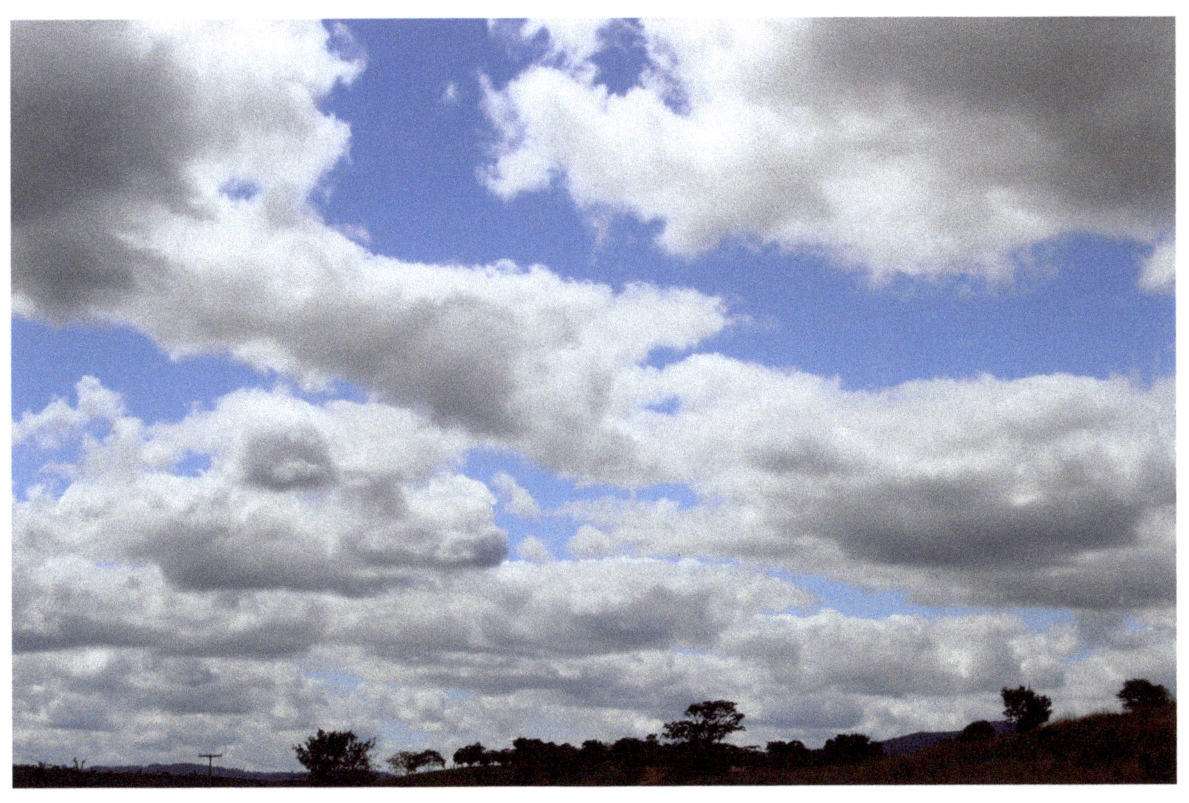

Sky Over Liberty Farm

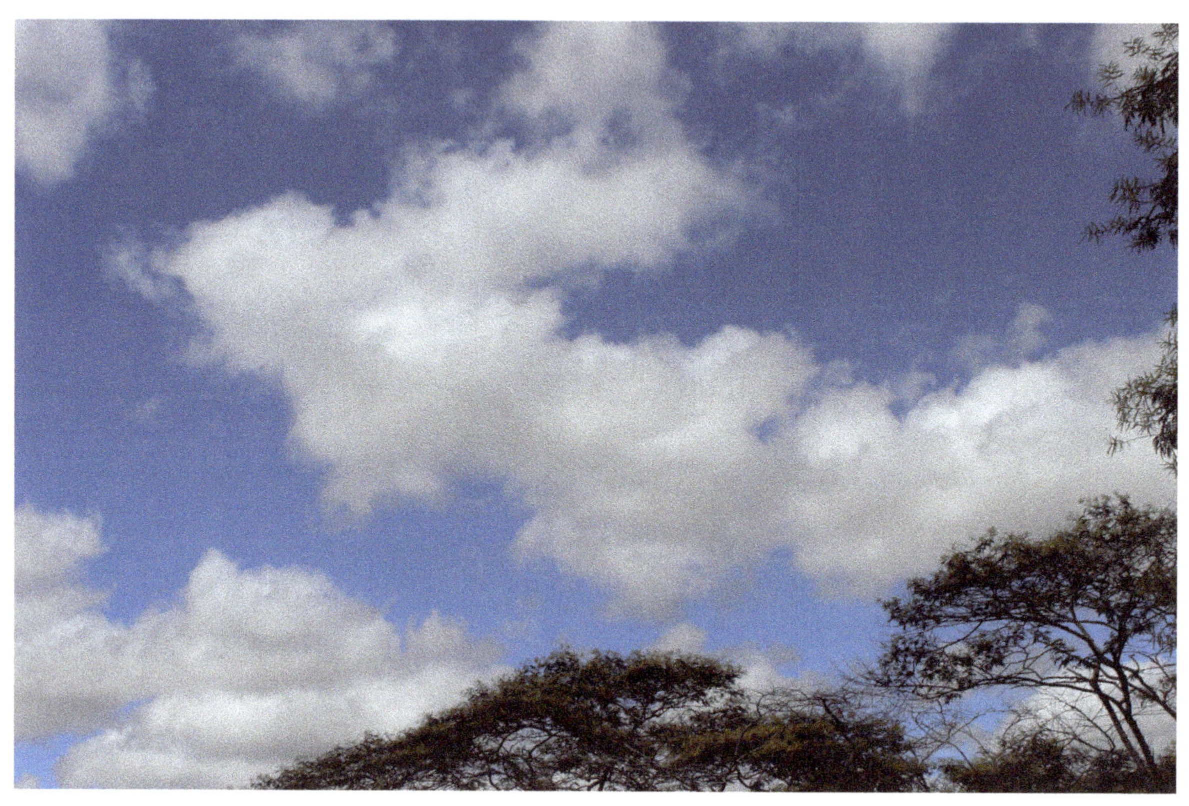

Izai Amorim

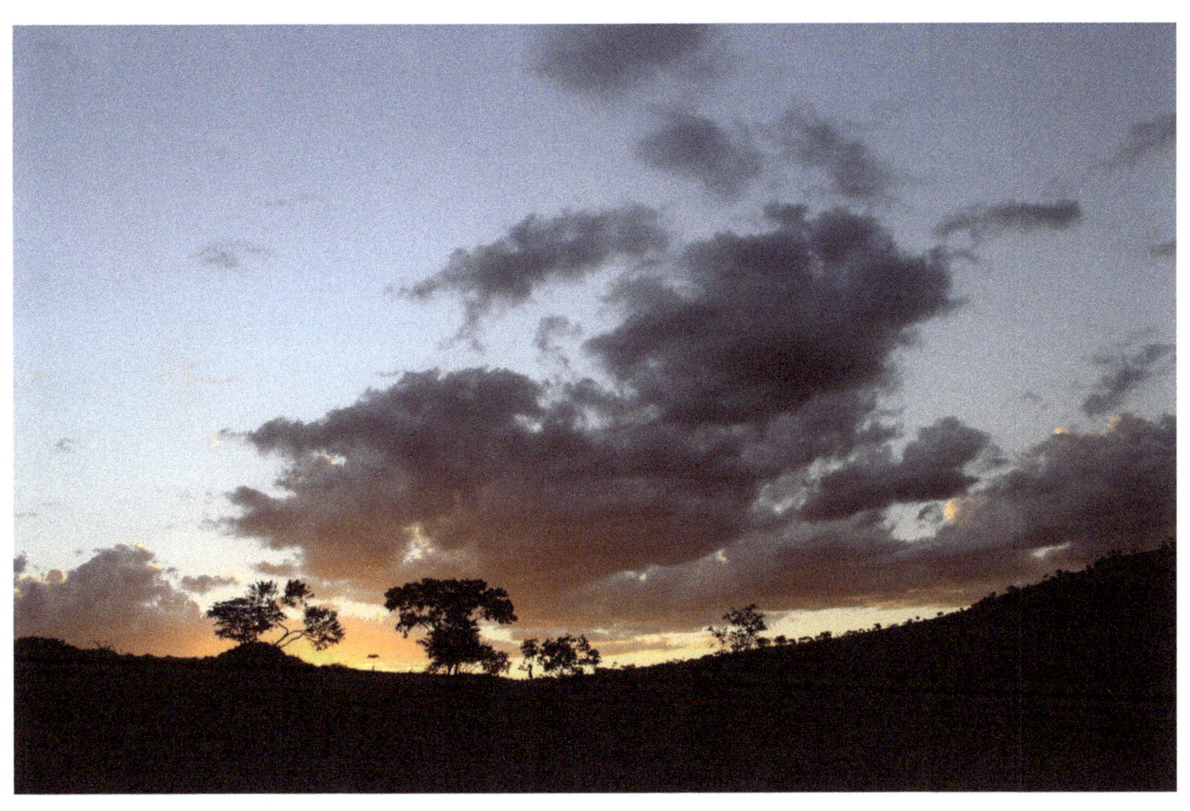

Sky Over Liberty Farm

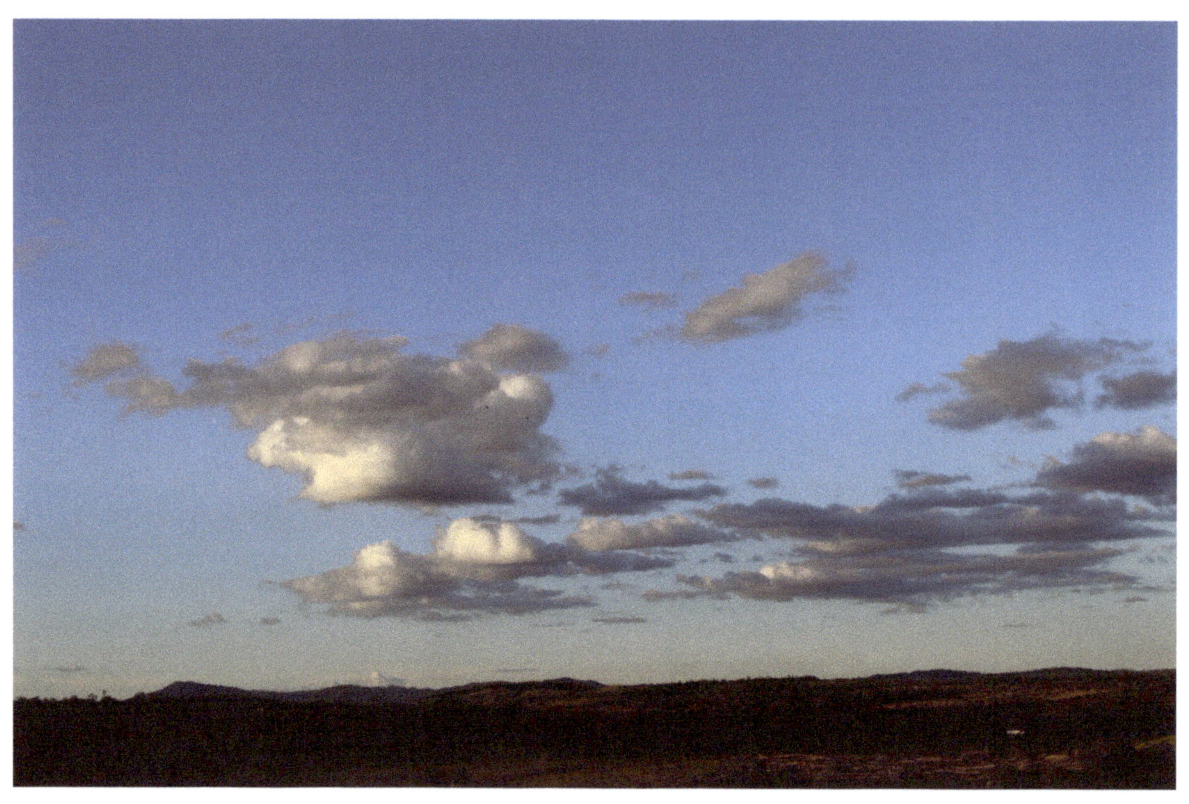

Izai Amorim

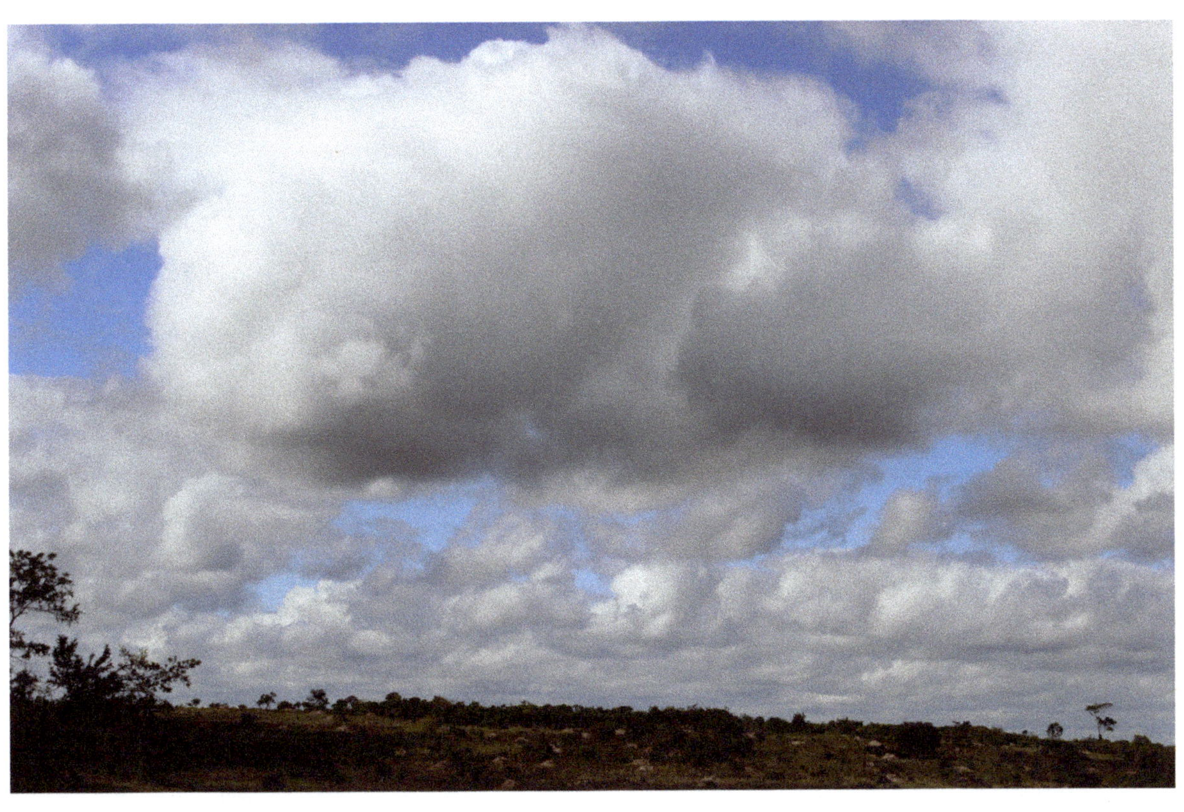

Sky Over Liberty Farm

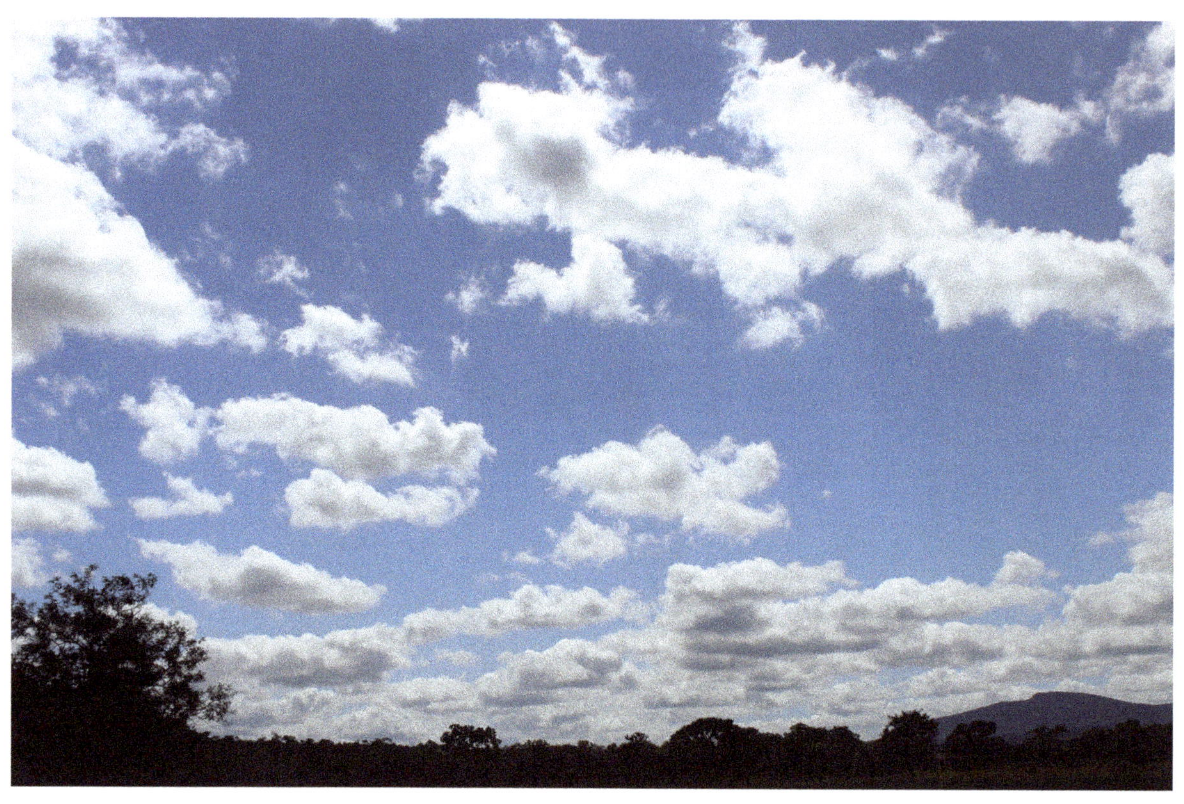

Izai Amorim

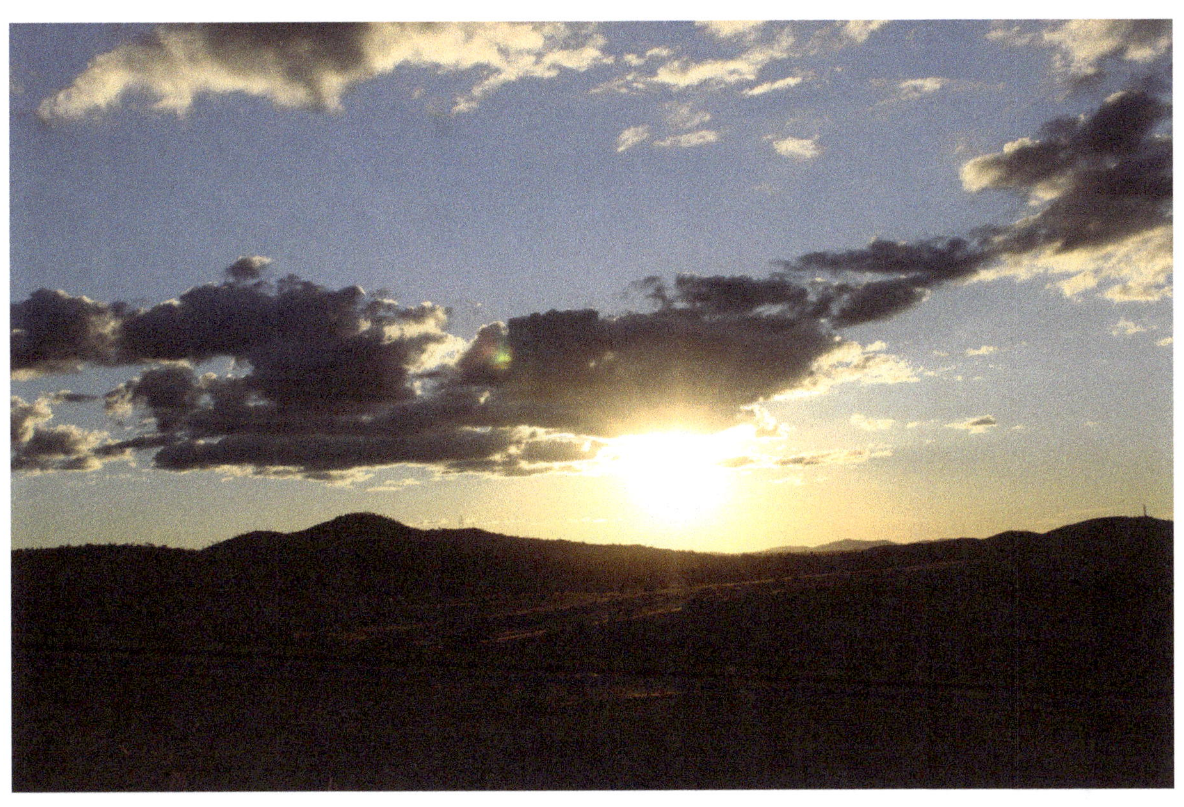

Sky Over Liberty Farm

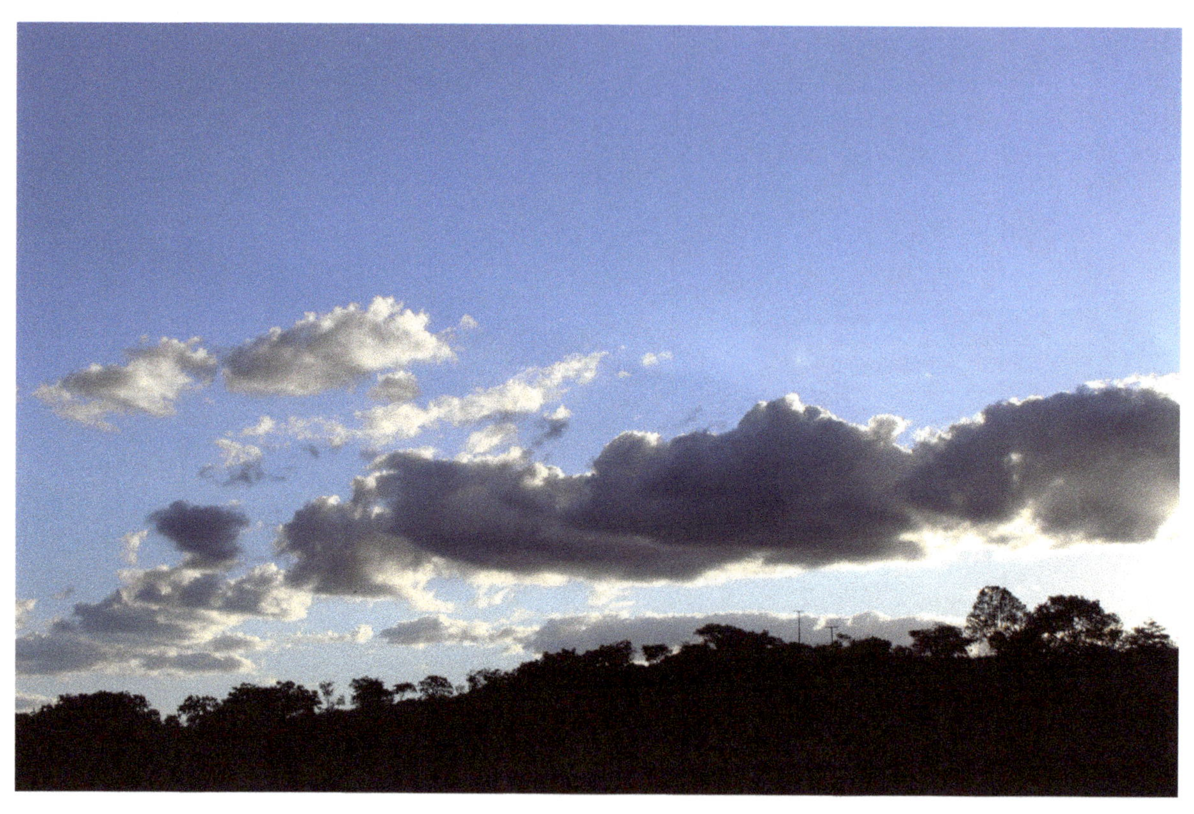

Izai Amorim

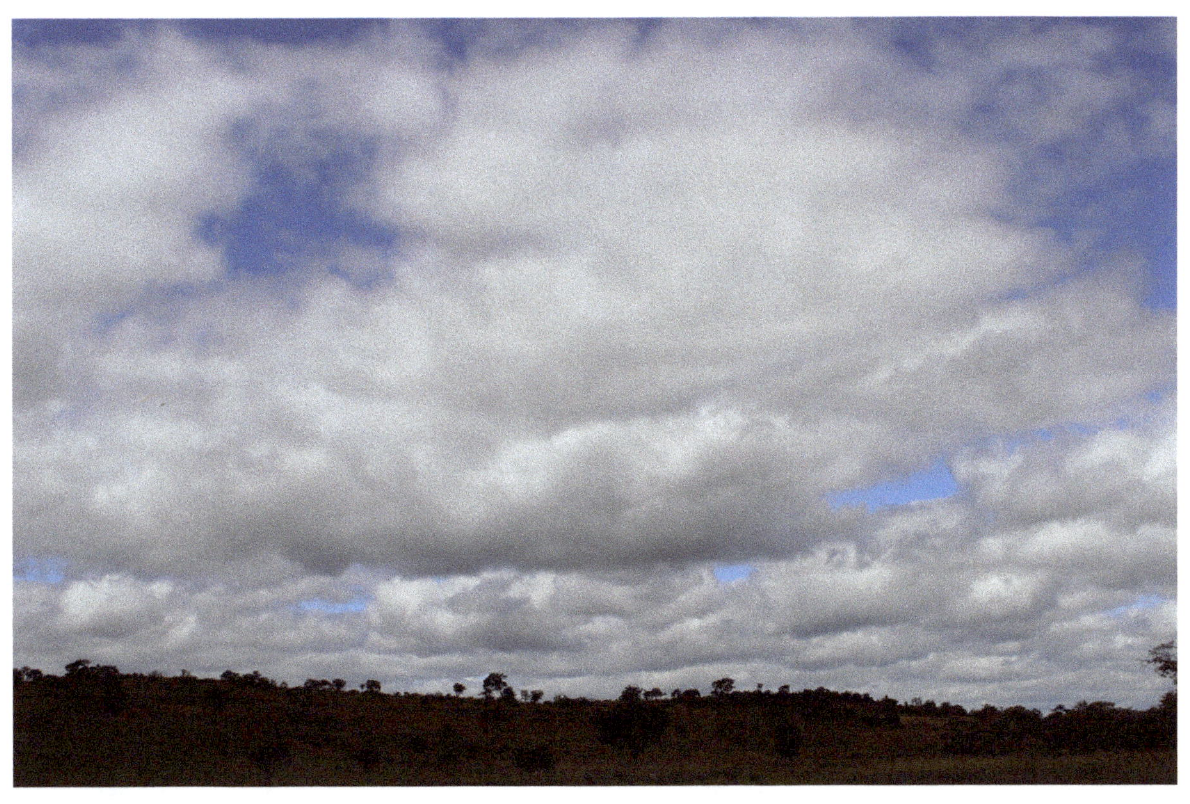

Sky Over Liberty Farm

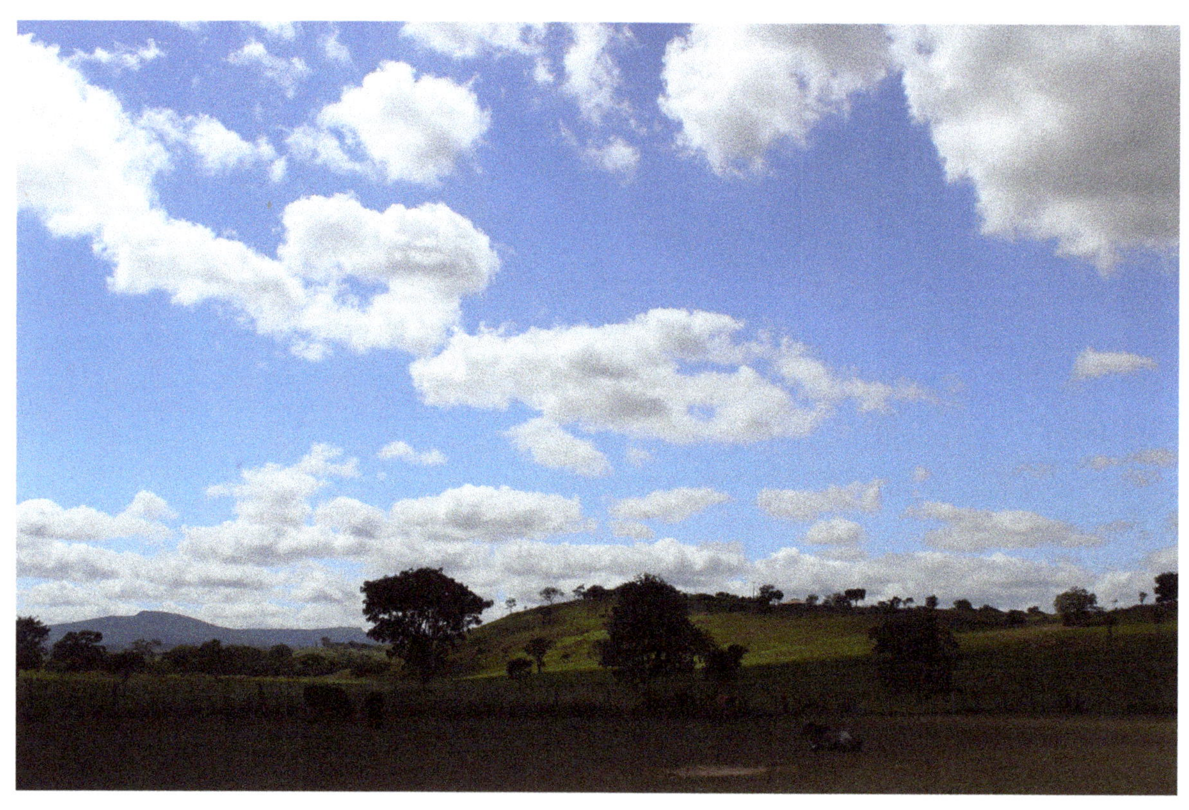

Izai Amorim

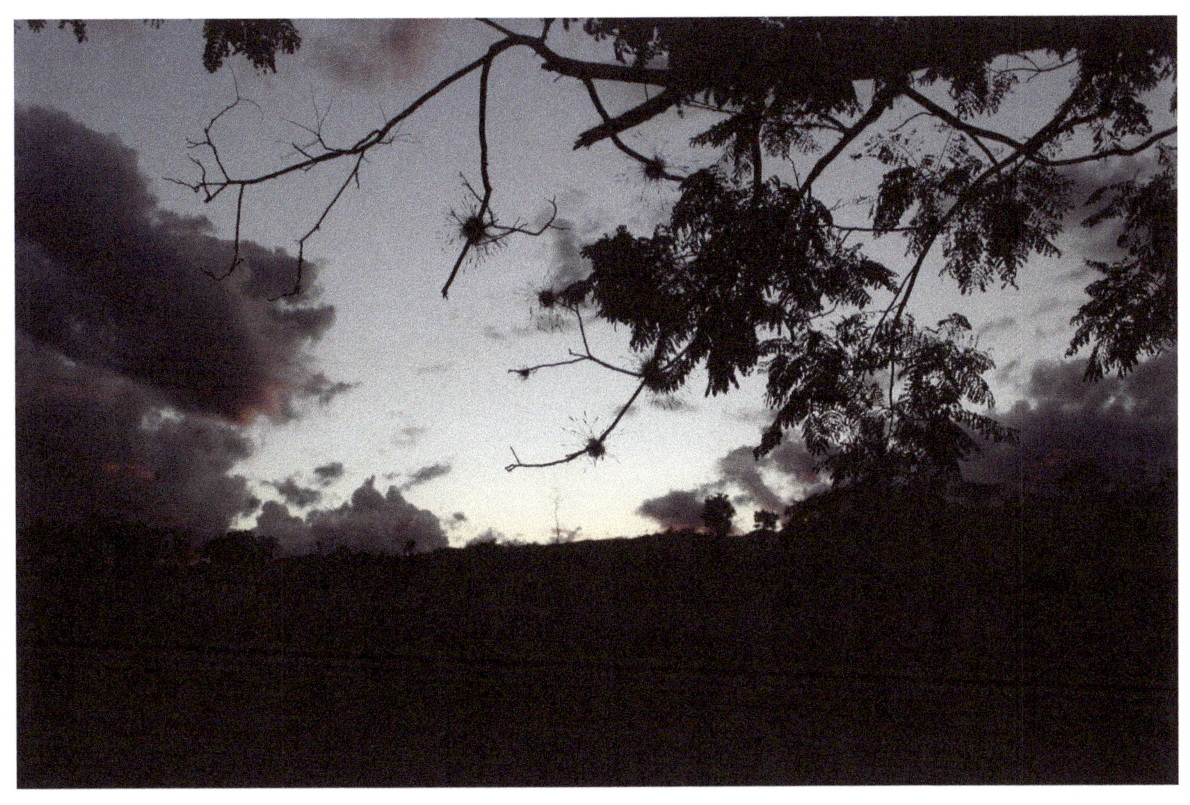

Sky Over Liberty Farm

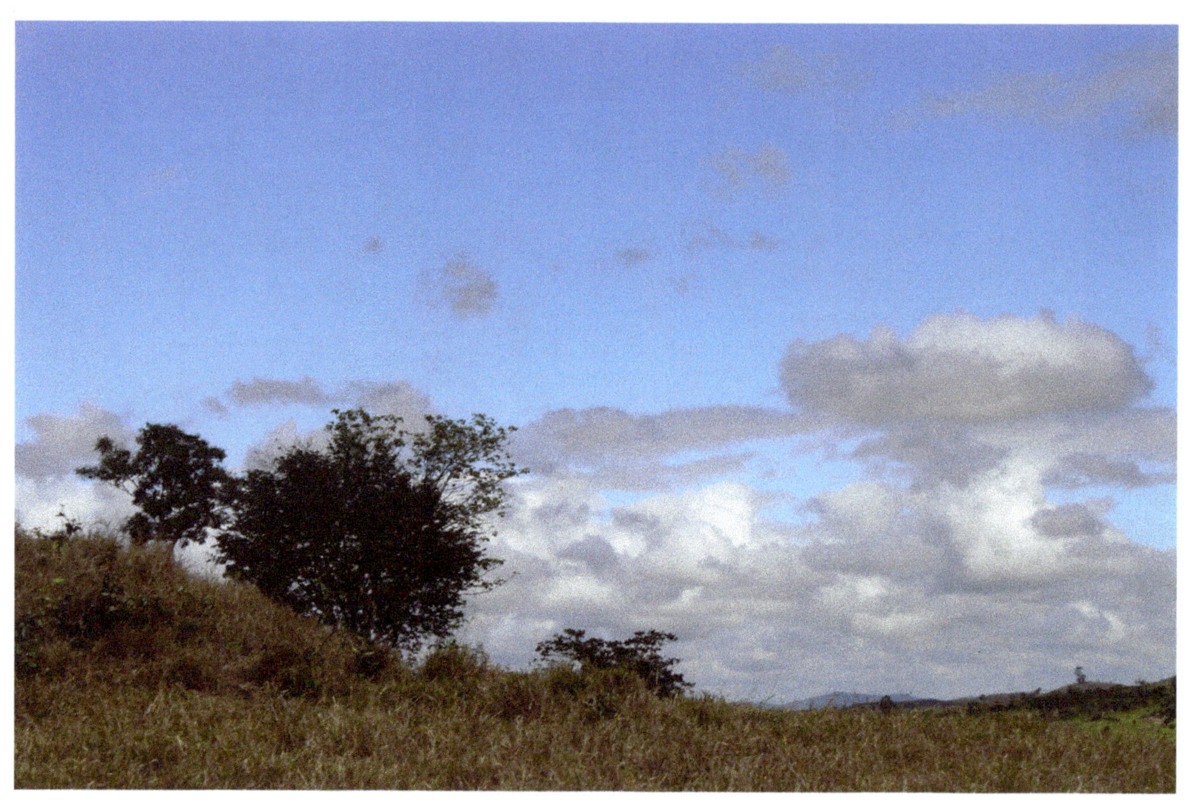

Izai Amorim

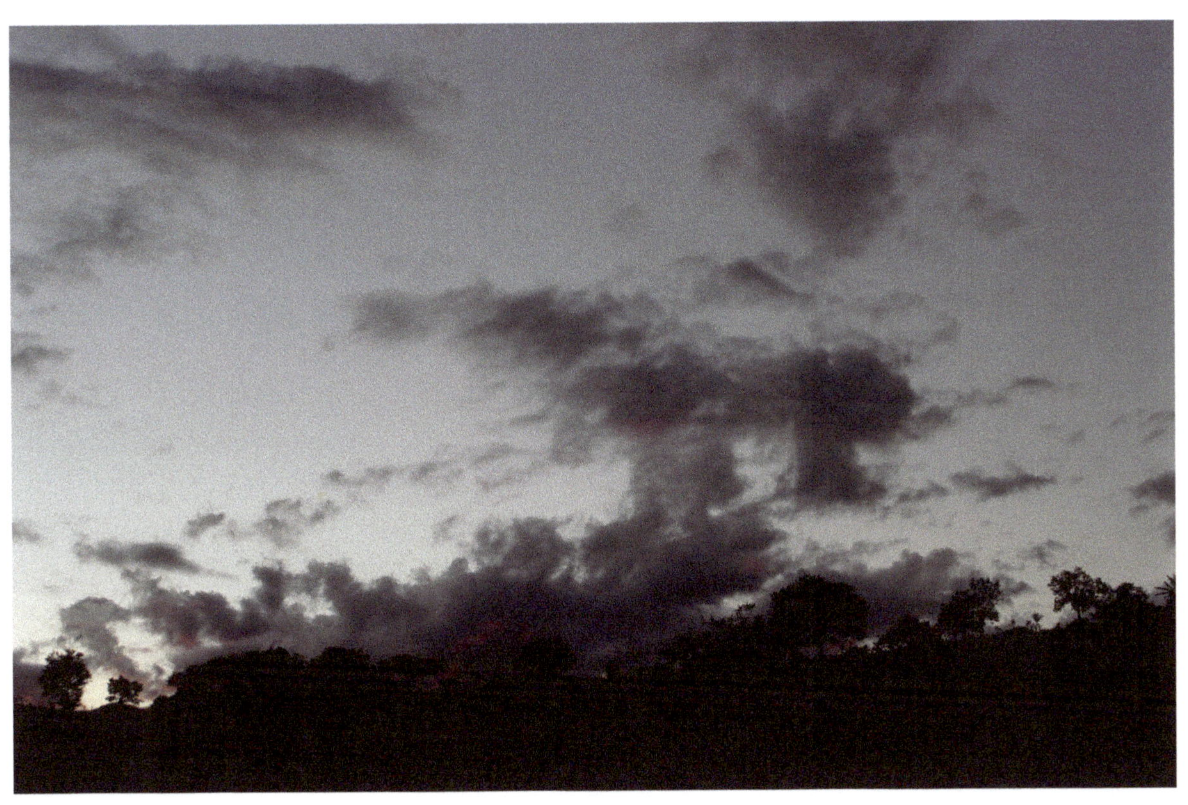

Sky Over Liberty Farm

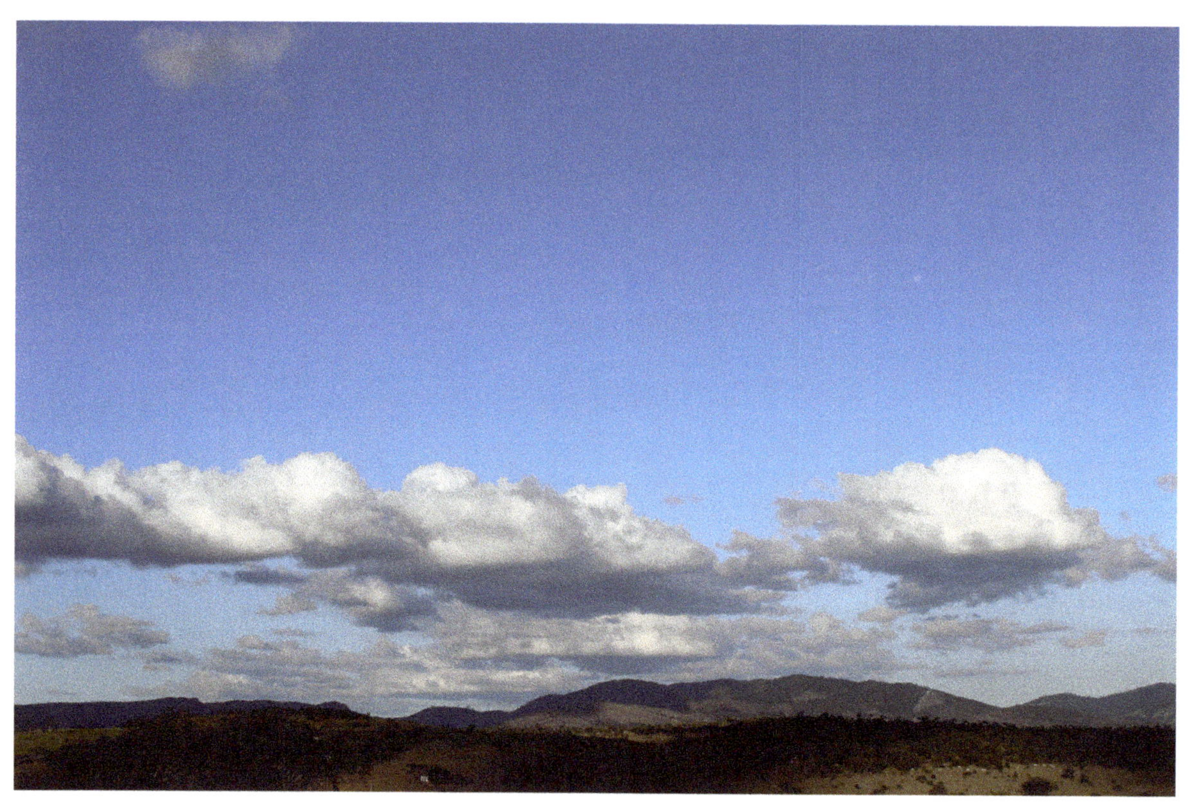

52

Izai Amorim

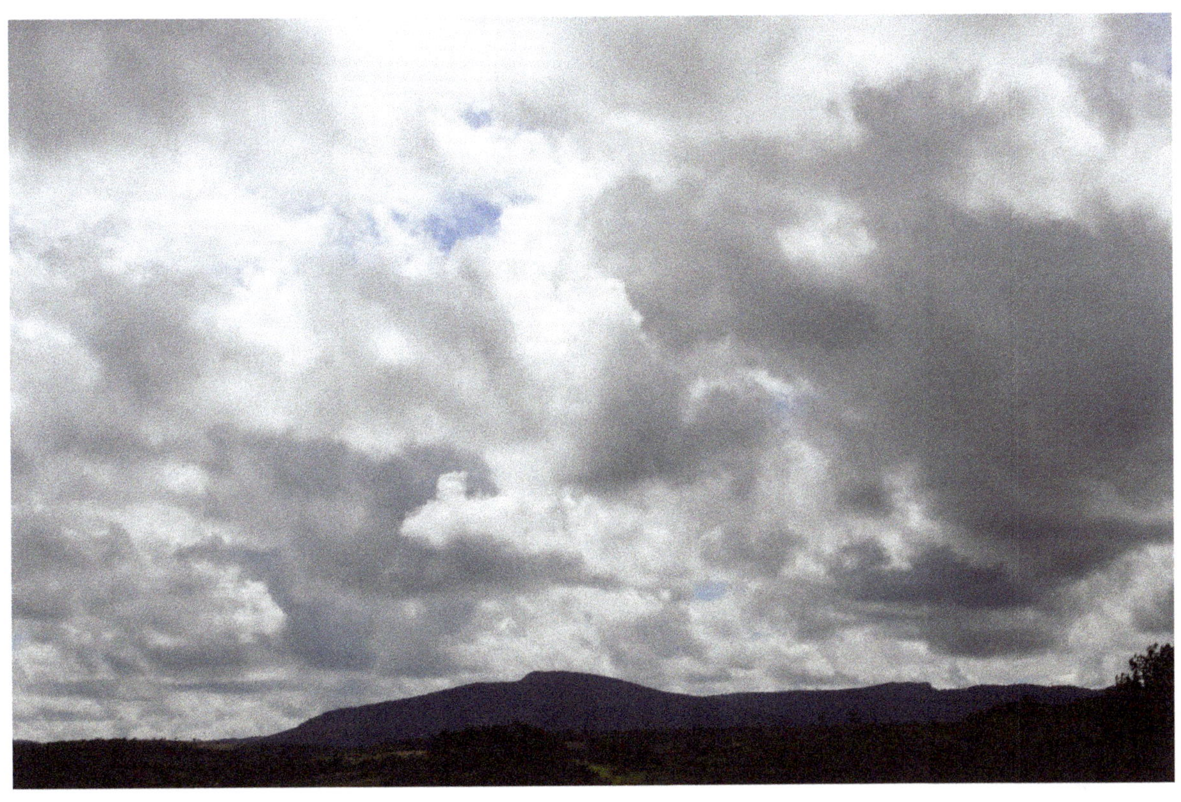

Sky Over Liberty Farm

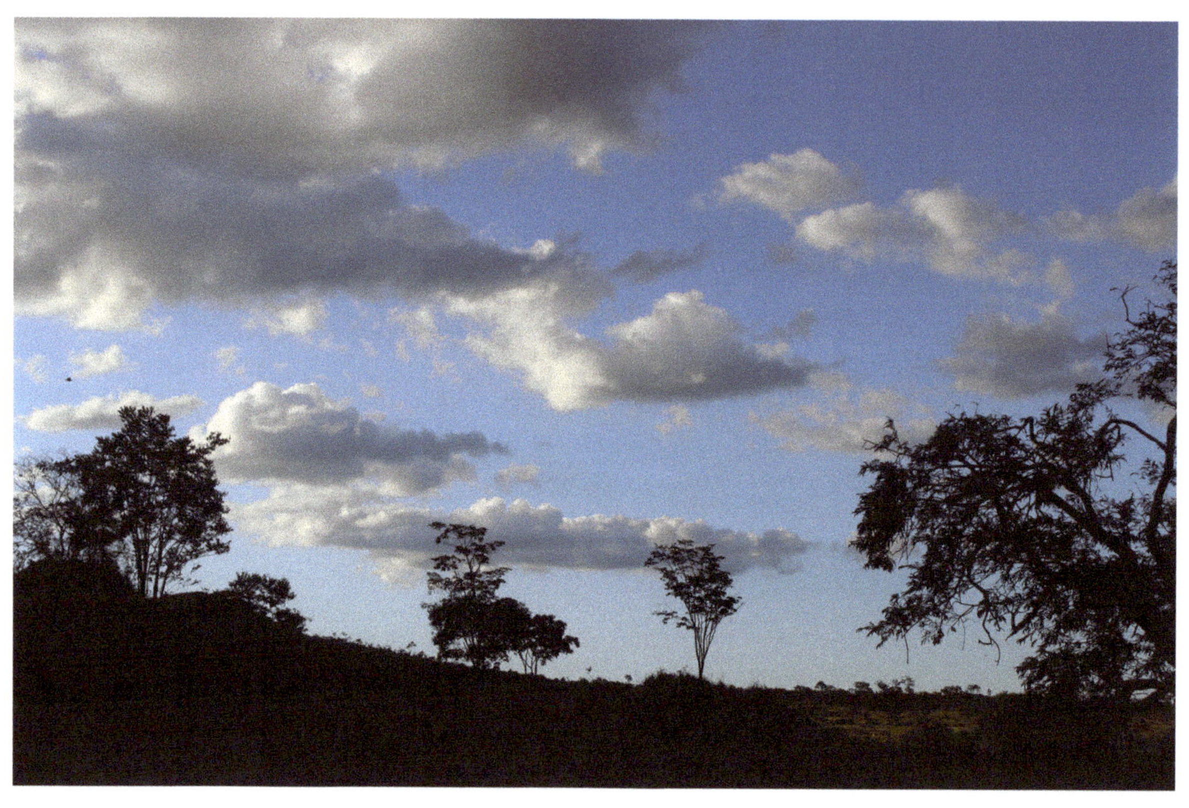

Izai Amorim

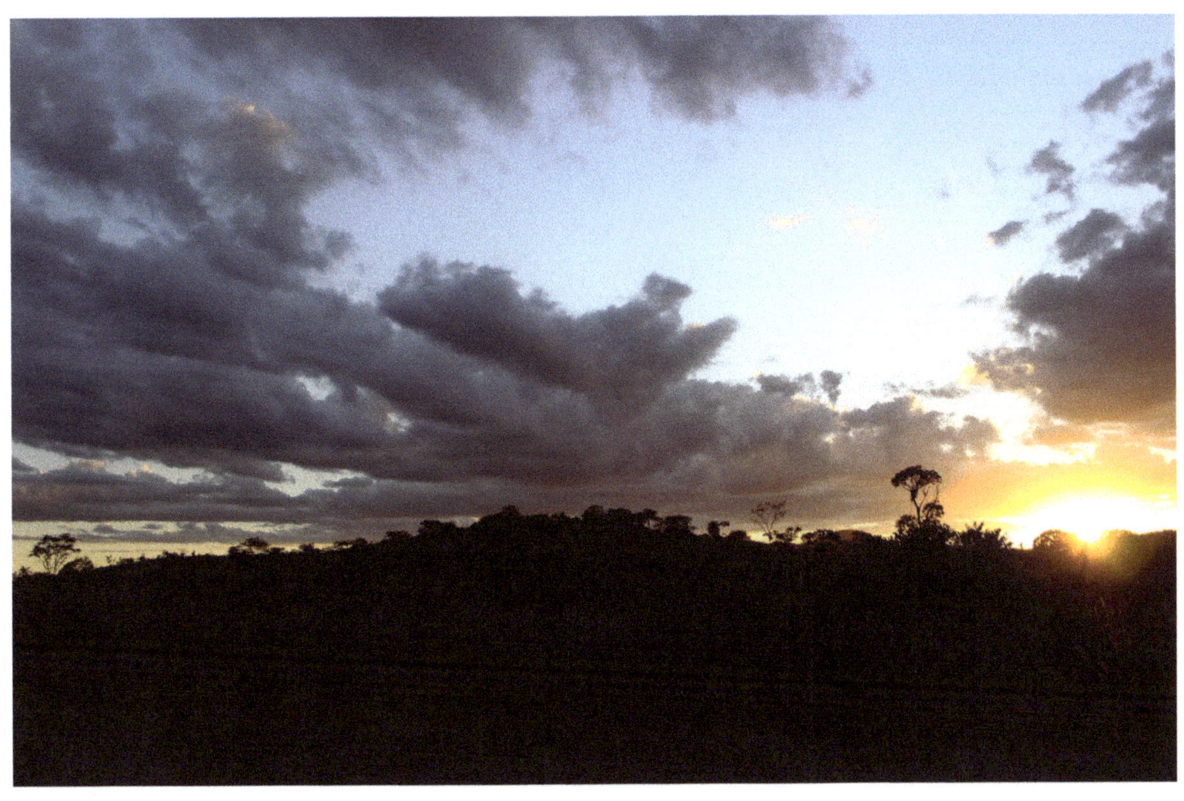

Sky Over Liberty Farm

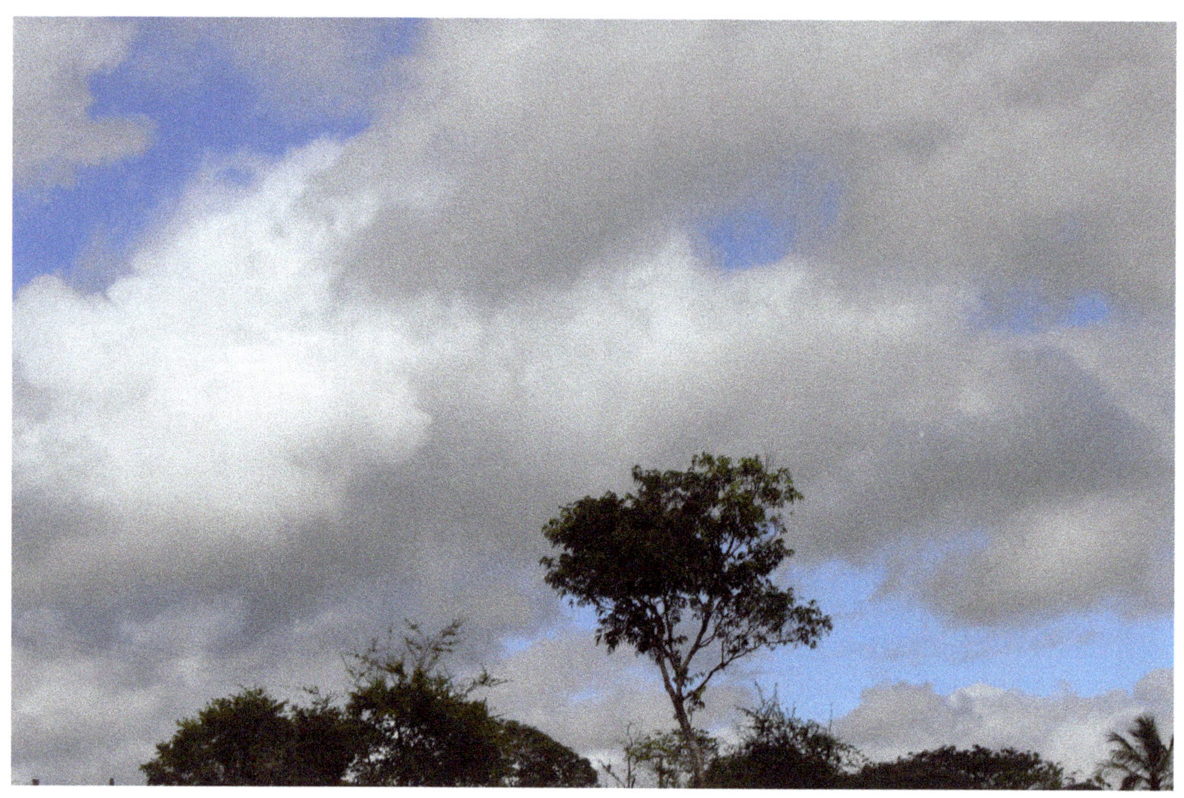

Izai Amorim

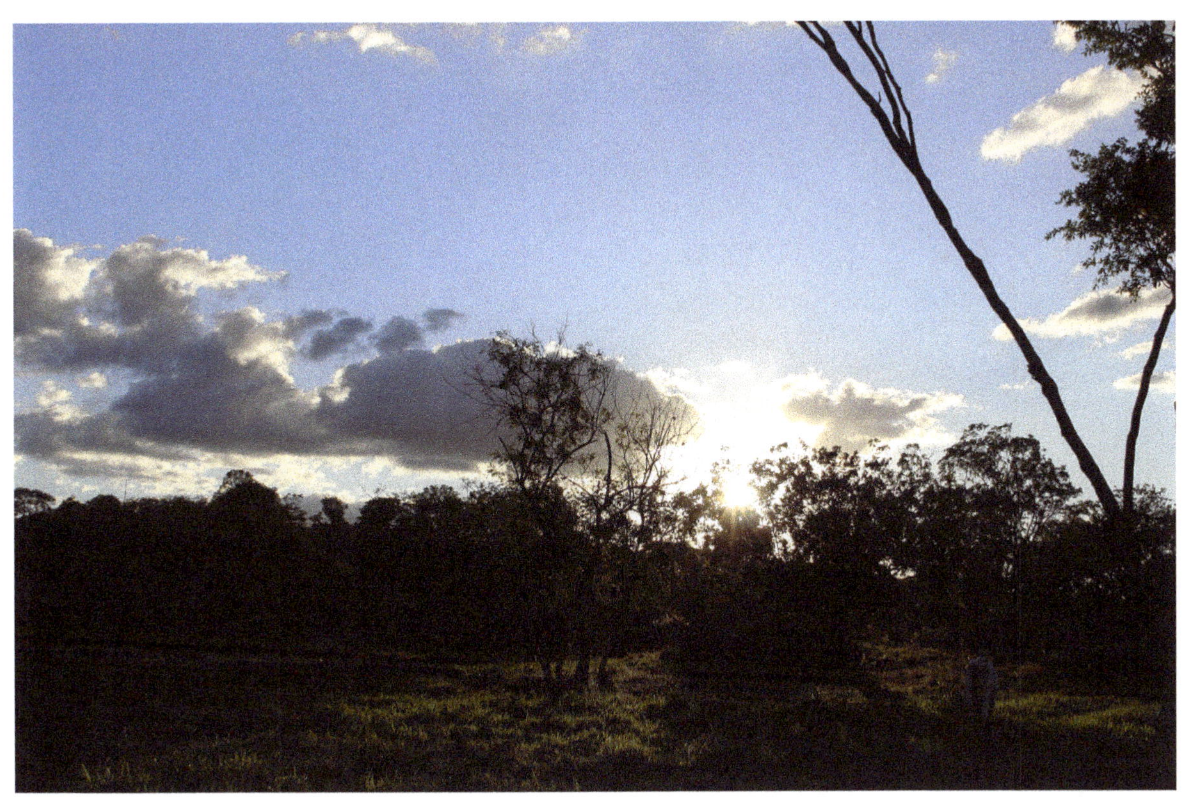

Sky Over Liberty Farm

Izai Amorim

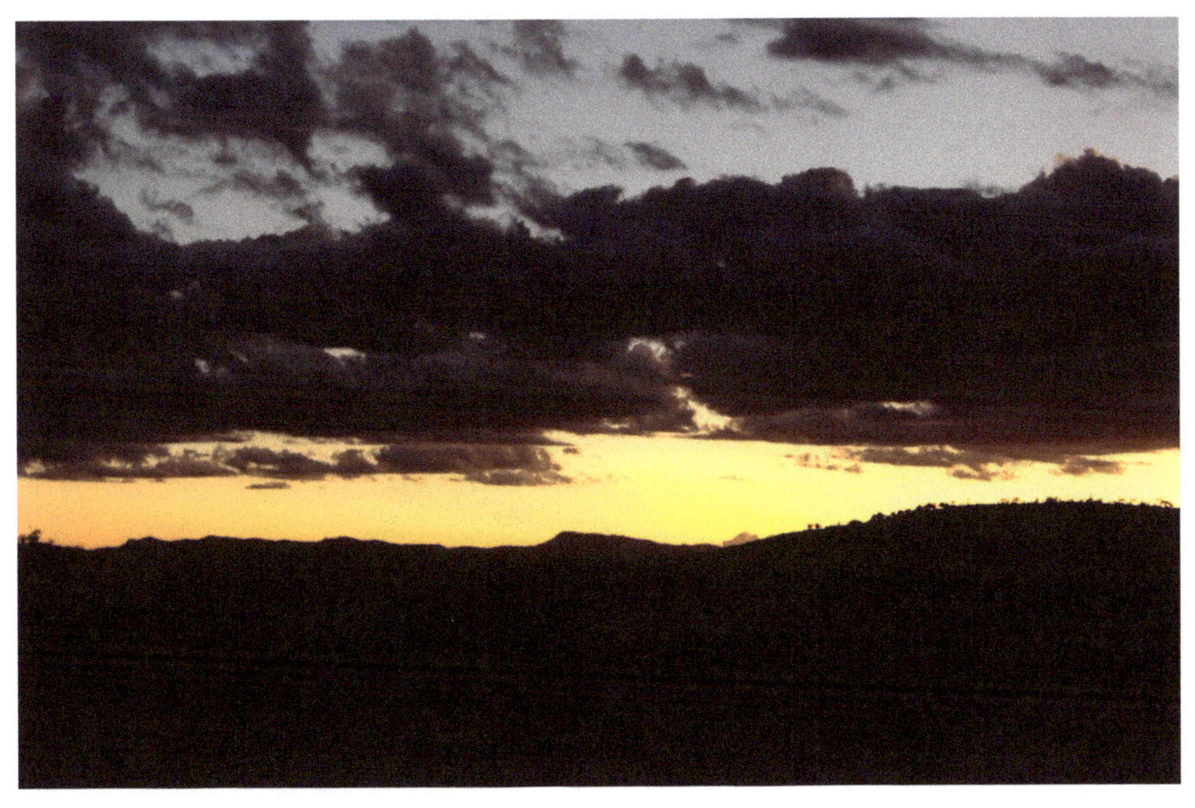

Sky Over Liberty Farm

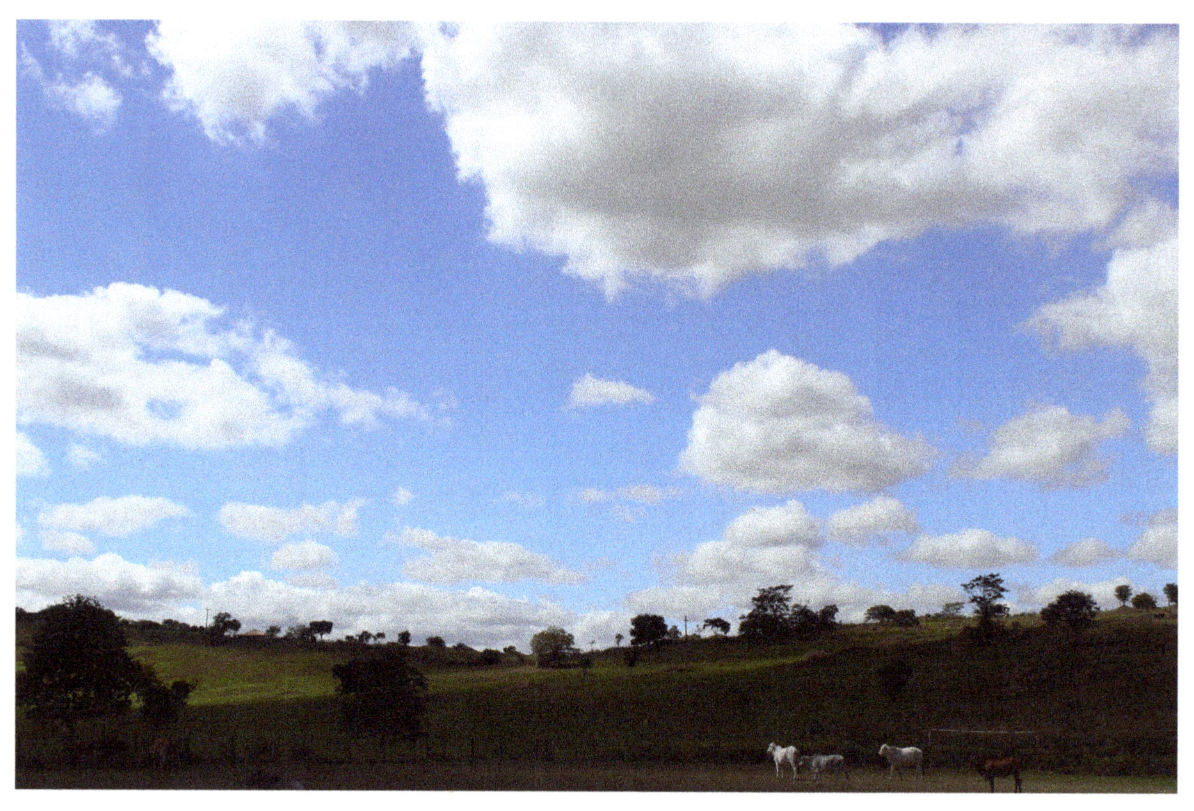

Izai Amorim